Sch...

TUDOR CHURCH MUSIC

Da Capo Press Music Reprint Series

TUDOR
CHURCH MUSIC.

By Denis Stevens

DA CAPO PRESS • NEW YORK • 1973

Library of Congress Cataloging in Publication Data

Stevens, Denis William, 1922-
    Tudor church music.

    (Da Capo Press music reprint series)
    Reprint of the ed. published by Merlin Press, New
York.
    1. Church music—England—History and criticism.
I. Title.
[ML2931.S8   1973]   783'.026'0942   73-4335
ISBN 0-306-70579-6

Published by Da Capo Press, Inc.
A Subsidiary of Plenum Publishing Corporation
227 West 17th Street, New York, N.Y. 10011

TUDOR CHURCH MUSIC

Tudor Church Music

DENIS STEVENS

MERLIN PRESS - NEW YORK

Copyright 1955. Merlin Press, Inc.

Manufactured in the United States of America.

THIS IS A MERLIN PRESS BOOK

OF THIS EDITION ONLY FIFTEEN HUNDRED
COPIES WERE MADE

THIS IS NUMBER ....

FOREWORD

Nearly forty years ago, the generosity of an American benefactor made possible the publication, in England, of a series of ten impressive volumes bearing the same title as this small and necessarily restricted study. Ten more volumes were projected, but never published, and although a number of octavo editions of separate works were issued, Mr. Andrew Carnegie's desire that music should reach the masses was unfortunately not realized, at least as far as Tudor Church Music was concerned.

Not only did the music not reach the masses, but in many cases it did not even reach that select band of scholars and aesthetes whose very lives were bound up with the study and practice of Tudor Church Music. Quite recently there have been several instances of the belated discovery of heavy packages, found to contain complete sets of the ten volumes, in ecclesiastical store-rooms of one kind or another. Thus the dust which scholars had carefully removed from centuries-old manuscripts was, with complete lack of concern, allowed to re-settle itself upon the wrappings of the published volumes. The music remained unsung (apart from the octavo editions already mentioned) and no attempt at stylistic criticism of the music, as an integral and important corpus, was even remotely thought of.

The present study does not set out to fill that gap. Extensive and plentiful musical examples would be a sine qua non of such a study. It has, however, been thought suitable to give as much relevant historical and liturgical information as space allows, since these aspects of the music provide us with significant clues regarding performance and interpretation. It is hoped that those whose interest in the period is aroused will seek out the music for themselves, and sing it, or sing it and play it, as the case may be.

It is my pleasant duty to thank Mr. Douglas Guest, Organist and Director of Music at Salisbury Cathedral, and Mr. Jeremy Noble, sometime Scholar of Worcester College, Oxford, for many helpful suggestions and criticisms. I am grateful also to my wife for her constant encouragement and her valuable assistance in the reading of typescript and proofs.

DENIS STEVENS.

HISTORY AND LITURGY

I

*T*HE CLOSING
years of the centuries-old rule of the House
of the Plantagenet saw a slow but inexor-
able decline in the stature of English polyphony. This noble art, which had achieved
so wide and so enviable a reputation during the reign of Henry V, suffered a mortal
blow in the year 1445, when Lionel Power
died in Canterbury. Eight years later the
death of John Dunstable closed forever a
glorious chapter in the history of English
liturgical music, and the Flemish theorist
and composer Johannes Tinctoris, sum-
ming up events at the moderately safe distance of twenty years or so, felt bound to
admit that the English had fallen from
their supreme position as inventors of new
techniques in music. In comparison with

the Franco-Flemish *avant-garde,* they did no more than "continue to use one and the same style of composition, which shows a lamentable lack of invention."

Indeed, the situation was rather akin to that which John Bossewell lamented a century later, when, in his *Workes of Armorie,* he thrusts before us this rhetorical question and answer: "But what saie I, Musicke? One of the seven Liberall sciences? It is almost banished this Realme." Yet the enthusiasm and devotion of a few men precluded its entire banishment, in the fifteenth century as in the sixteenth. The craft, as well as the spirit, of the careful and colourful scribes of the Old Hall and Egerton manuscripts was to live on in those who limned the great choirbooks of Eton, Lambeth, and Cambridge. Musicians, no less than scribes, gained new heart and courage when Henry VII, the first monarch of the new Tudor dynasty, was crowned on November 7, 1485.

Henry, as a Lancastrian, had a weak

hereditary claim to the throne, but his marriage to Elizabeth of York did much to reconcile the opposing faction, and before long both government and treasury began to flourish. The royal marriage called forth musical tributes from two composers who were later to make their mark as distinguished writers of liturgical polyphony: Thomas Ashwell and Gilbert Banester. The former is credited with an anthem, apparently not now extant, beginning with the words "God save King Harry." If the anthem really did exist, Ashwell's Mass of the same title (partially preserved in St. John's College and the University Library, Cambridge) would qualify as the earliest Tudor example of a parody Mass: otherwise it must be dismissed as a musicological mirage.

Banester's motet *O Maria et Elizabeth* is far more tangible, and is still to be seen today in the fine choirbook preserved in the library at Eton College. It contains a prayer which reads "protege quesumus tibi

devotum athletam regem nostrum," and
although no name is given by the scribe,
there is little doubt as to the identity of
the monarch, for Banester died in 1487,
only two years after Henry's coronation.
The comparatively infrequent use of five-
part harmony for full choir seems to give
the motet an aura of austere strength.

One other work deserves to be mentioned in connection with occasional or ceremonial music during Henry VII's reign,
and that is the motet *Aeterne laudis lilium*
by Robert Fayrfax. Elizabeth herself appears to have commissioned the motet, for
her Privy Purse expenses for the year 1502
make mention of a payment to Fayrfax
"for setting an anthem of our Lady and
Saint Elizabeth." The name of the saint—
and of the queen—is given great musical
prominence towards the end of the work,
and may well have been intended as a royal
compliment.

Ceremonial music aside, there was much
for composers to exercise their minds upon

in the widespread and complex Sarum liturgy. Although Salisbury was its rightful home, and the eleventh century Rouen ritual its corner-stone, it came to be regarded as the official liturgy in the greater part of England, even of the British isles. True enough, there was a Use of Hereford, of Bangor, of York, and of Lincoln (though traces of this last have all but disappeared)—yet they varied only slightly from the main source and fountain-head of their inspiration. The elaborate and imposing ceremonial of High Mass called for music of corresponding dignity and equivalent complexity, while the daily Office (especially Matins and Vespers) was in constant need of solemn settings of antiphons, hymns, responsories, and canticles.

High Mass, according to a Sarum rubric (and to current Roman practice), should be celebrated after Terce on Sundays and the principal Feasts, after Sext on weekdays and lesser Feasts, and after None during Advent, Lent, and Vigils. The actual time of the day varied, of course, with the time of the year; but it may easily be seen that a composer or singer serving a large ecclesiastical establishment, whether Abbey, Cathedral, or Chapel Royal, could be expected to take his proper part in the liturgy at any time during the day. In many cases he would compose the music asked of him by the Precentor, rehearse it with the members of the choir, and sing in it (whilst directing from his stall) when the service was celebrated.

How he came to compose it is a question which has long interested musicians and scholars, for they realize only too well that the choirbook (with separate voice-parts on adjacent pages) and the part-books which flourished at a later date, represent only the final version of the music. It might have existed in score before it was copied out according to its component voice-parts. Yet scores had little attraction for musicians of the Renaissance. An exactly corresponding situation may be seen in the vocal and instrumental music of the Baroque era: then, as in earlier days, a first violinist or continuo player would set the tempo and change it when necessary. In Tudor times, the choirmaster would set the tempo and attend to the details of performance: a score would have been both a luxury and a hindrance.

The Precentor, at the beginning of every week, wrote the names of those entrusted with special duties in the ceremony, on a waxed board which was hung up in the chapter-house for all to see. At the end of the week, the wax was smoothed over and inscribed upon once more. This is almost certainly the way in which composers wrote their music: valuable parchment and paper were not wasted in rough drafts, and alterations were easy to make. Architects too used waxed boards for their plans; this explains the lack of detailed plans for buildings erected during the Middle Ages. Instead of blueprints and scores, we have cathedrals and choirbooks.

11

The entire reign of Henry VII and the greater part of Henry VIII's reign saw no major liturgical changes. Composers were thus able to build up a strong tradition in form and texture, and it is largely due to this tradition that the salient characteristics of English polyphony were preserved, in one way or another, until the very end of the century. In matters of form, the liturgy itself was of prime importance by virtue of its wide and almost uniform currency. Texture, however, was a more variable factor, depending for the most part upon the number and type of singers available. Most of the larger abbeys and cathedrals, and not a few collegiate churches of the size of Eton or King's College Cambridge, possessed choirs of twenty or more voices. Even a body of sixteen singers was a useful, sonorous, and eminently practical asset to the liturgy, for the fashionable norm in texture was five actual voice-parts. Most of Fayrfax's music is in five parts, and if his motet *O bone Jesu* were still complete it would

12

almost certainly be written for this disposition of vocal resources, as in the case of the parody Mass based upon it. A nearly contemporary setting of the same text, however, shows us that the density of texture could be four times as great as that used by Fayrfax. The composer of this setting, which contains acclamations written in as many as nineteen real voice-parts, is the Scottish priest Robert Carver, sometime canon of Scone Abbey in Perthshire.

A famous medieval description of the love of part-singing in Wales might easily tempt us to trace an equally strong love of music in certain Tudor monarchs to this very same source. Both Henry VIII and Queen Elizabeth were musically gifted: of the former, Henry Peacham tells us in *The Compleat Gentleman* that he "could not onely sing his part sure, but of himselfe compose a Service of four, five, and sixe parts; as Erasmus in a certaine Epistle, testifieth of his own knowledge." Many of Henry's compositions have come down to us, as well as works written in his honour. The motet *Quam pulchra es,* which is ascribed to Henry in the Baldwin manuscript, shows considerable skill in the manipulation of three voice-parts (two tenors and bass), besides a sure grasp of the intricacies of mensural proportions. A musical cleric who enjoyed preferment as well as protection, thanks to royal interest, was Richard Sampson; and it is by no means surprising to discover him as composer— and perhaps author too—of a long motet in praise of King Henry: *Psallite felices protecti culmine rose purpuree.* A prayer for Henry is to be found in a short motet *Christe Jesu pastor bone,* by John Taverner, who used some of the musical material, parody-wise, in his Mass *Small Devotion.*

An ill-controlled temperament allied with a constant anxiety over the succession caused the annulment of Henry's marriage with Catherine of Aragon, and the sentence of excommunication pronounced by

14

Pope Clement VII in 1533. The names of many church musicians may be seen among the vast number of ecclesiastical subscribers and signatories to the Act of Supremacy passed in June of the following year. In acknowledging Henry as the supreme head of the English Church, the musicians, in company with all the other church dignitaries, helped to create a liturgical *impasse* which was not to be finally disposed of until the Act of Uniformity of 1662, during the reign of Charles II. Shortly after 1535 composers began to experiment with musical settings of Marshall's English version of the Sarum *Horae;* in 1539, the year of the "Great Bible," Hilsey's *Prymer* succeeded Marshall's. Henry VIII's *Prymer,* published in 1545, led the way to the first Book of Common Prayer ratified in 1549 by the first Act of Uniformity. To add to this confusion over texts to be set to music, there was confusion in the very ranks of musicians themselves, for the dissolution of monasteries and abbey churches between

1535 and 1540 resulted in a widespread re-distribution of musical talent throughout the whole of England. There is no doubt that the finest of the musicians were quickly absorbed into the changing framework of the English church, though for many of them the change must have meant a temporary loss of prestige, though not necessarily a loss of salary.

Perhaps the most remarkable feature of Tudor music is the expression of artistic continuity which it so often reveals to the student and listener. Although it is not entirely a continuity of idiom, it possesses an underlying mood and feeling which stamps it as English and therefore as insular. The achievements of the most outstanding among Italian and Franco-Belgian composers were known and respected in well-informed English musical circles; but those same circles, catholic in both outlook and religion, jealously guarded the finer points of style which eventually set them in a class by themselves. An Italian visitor to Henry

VIII's court described the singing of the choristers during High Mass as "more divine than human," and of the basses (whose range is admirably portrayed by the choice of the word *contrabbassi*) he admitted that "they probably have not their equals in the whole world."

That account, written in 1515, may profitably be compared with another (this time from the pen of a German visitor) much later in the century. The place was Windsor; the occasion was morning service in St. George's Chapel: "the music, especially the organ, was exquisitely played, for at times you could hear the sound of cornetts, flutes, then fifes and other instruments; and there was likewise a little boy who sang so sweetly amongst it all, and threw such a charm over the music with his little tongue, that it was really wonderful to listen to him." Many years after, Captain Cooke of the Chapel Royal was to use cornetts to double his singers, but mainly in order to keep them in tune, for they became sadly

17

out of practice during the Commonwealth. No such stunting of musical talent can be laid at the door of the Reformation, however, and the continuity, of choral excellence which is apparent in the continental tributes just quoted, went hand in hand with a similar flow of creative activity.

Composers were not, as a rule, unwilling to set English words to music. They did so as a matter of course in their court-songs, part-songs, and madrigals. Para-liturgical forms including carols for Christmas, Easter, and other feasts had been closely bound up with the vernacular since the middle of the fifteenth century, and it had even become fashionable to mix Latin and English texts. An example of this macaronic procedure as applied to a setting of the canticle *Te Deum* may be seen in the composition by Thomas Packe. An ostensibly normal opening verse, with the cantor's intonation answered by five-part polyphony, is followed immediately by an English gloss: "We praise the, almighty god; we

knowlych the oure mercyfulle lord." There-
after odd Latin words appear in the midst
of the English text, with the complete
phrase "Te Dominum confitemur" coming
round as a chorus at the end of every verse.

The real difficulty about setting the texts
of the various Prymers was not a religious
one, but a musical difficulty born of Cranmerian contortions. It was Cranmer who
first confused the musico-liturgical func-
tions of homophony and polyphony; and it
is much to the credit of Tudor composers that they extracted themselves so effec-
tively from the chains he sought to throw
about them. The sequences and proses of
the Sarum rite, together with hymns and
special prayers set by musicians in con-
ductus style, all agreed fundamentally with
Cranmer's precepts for the new style of
church music—that is, not "full of notes,
[melismatic] but, as near as may be, for
every syllable a note." One might add
"for every two syllables a step," since the
sequences were meant to be sung during

procession, and their function was to provide a steady and dignified rhythmic pulse. Cranmer seized this simple and rhythmical style of writing and proceeded to apply it to non-processional activities, to which it was obviously not suited. Since processions came to be frowned upon as superstitious and unnecessary, and the Litany itself was sung in procession only very rarely (as at Rogationtide), it is not surprising that the projected English version of the Latin *Processionale* came to nothing. Composers did indeed try to simplify their part-writing, and there is no doubt that their efforts had a welcome, if astringent, effect upon Elizabethan style; but they could no more inspire themselves with an anthem sounding like a slow-motion frottola than their architectural colleagues could abide a return to quadripartite vaulting after having perfected in stone the miraculous counterpoint of tierceron and lierne.

The Bodleian manuscripts known as the Wanley part-books (after a former owner) exemplify the many different cross-currents of musical thought and texture which existed side by side during the last decade of Henry VIII's reign. But only two out of ten Communion services can be said to follow Cranmer's sober and solemn injunctions: of the remaining eight, four are not unduly florid, while the other four are distinctly so. Two of the florid settings are adaptations, probably by the composer himself, of the Masses *Sine Nomine* and *Small Devotion* by John Taverner, who—however much he may have repented of his "Popish ditties"—yet found it convenient to retain the ditty and substitute only a new verbal text. Thus, in spite of recurring objections, the Tudor composers continued in their understandable reluctance to abandon the horizontal aspect of musical texture, and their stubborn attitude bore healthy fruit in later years.

The closely inter-related affairs of church and state gave rise to an increased number of prayers for the King, ranging

from a simple clause in the 1544 Litany
to an elaborate eight-part setting of a
prayer for Edward VI. Two syllabic and
four-part Litanies appear in the Wanley manuscripts, and they both use, or
rather fit (for the tenor part-book is missing) the plainsong which Cranmer issued
with his Litany. England being then at war
with Scotland, and in a state of prepara-
tion for war with France, special prayers
are asked for the King's Majesty "who at
this presente tyme hath taken upon him the
great and daungerous affayres of warre."

When the youthful Edward VI acceded
to the throne in 1547, plans were already
in hand to enforce the reading of Epistle
and Gospel in English during High Mass.
The plans were ratified in the royal Injunctions, which also expressly forbade processions. Injunctions delivered in the following
year to the Dean and Chapter of Lincoln Cathedral demanded of them that
"they shall from henceforth sing or say no
anthem of our Lady or other Saints, but

22

only of our Lord, and then not in Latin; but choosing out the best and most sounding to Christian religion they shall turn the same into English, setting thereunto a plain and distinct note for every syllable one; they shall sing them and none other." The anti-Marian feeling was thus gradually intensified; and Tudor composers lost what was perhaps one of their most characteristically intimate forms of devotion—the motet in honour of the Blessed Virgin.

Early in 1549, the London printers Grafton and Whitchurch were busily engaged in printing the First Book of Common Prayer, which was ordered to be used exclusively in all churches throughout the land on and after Whitsun Day, June 9. It was not well received by church dignitaries, most of whom considered that it should undergo further, and even drastic reform, before being wholeheartedly adopted. Composers therefore were still in the awkward state of not knowing for certain whether the liturgy would survive, and

it is not surprising that they turned their
energies to the setting of anthems, such as
those contained in the (incomplete) set of
Edwardian part-books in the British Museum. Here, as in the Wanley part-books,
most of the compositions are anonymous:
it is almost as if anonymity in this time of
musical experiment were a kind of cloak
with which to hide the current utilitarian
apparel. The prayer for Edward may well
have been written in July or August of
1549, shortly before yet another declara-
tion of war upon the French: "O lorde
Christe Jesu that art kyng in glory and
very perfit roote of all our felicity, we sin-
ners do most humbly beseech thy hy majesty to graunt thy noble servant our sove-
reign lorde kyng Edward, that he may have
thorough thee ovyr all his enemies most
ryall victory . . ."

In 1553 Edward died of consumption,
and the Reformation which had made
such headway under the aegis of the Pro-
tector, Somerset, suffered a temporary

though violent reverse at the hands of Queen Mary. It was during her reign that Philip of Spain and his court paid a visit to England, and there still exist accurate accounts of the royal meeting at Winchester, where all attended High Mass in the cathedral. Although Antonio de Cabezon, in charge of Philip's musicians, was then at the height of his powers as a composer and organist, it is extremely doubtful whether he had any direct influence on English music of the time. In the first place, the political atmosphere was far too unsettled for any real *rapprochement* between musicians of the English and Spanish chapels. The stern measures adopted by Mary must have done much toward alienating her subjects from the retinue of her guests, and an unpopular and childless marriage did not help matters. In the second place, the music which was published by Henestrosa in 1557 does not show Cabezon in a very favourable light, though it proves that he was a composer of taste

25

and one whose sense of liturgical values was impeccable. But in the field of virtuosity, experiment, and ideas, the English organists (whose works have unfortunately not been published in anything like their entirety) are far and away superior to the Spaniard, and it is clear from their highly individual style that they could have learnt little from even the greatest of continental keyboard players.

John Barnard, who in 1641 was the first ever to print an anthology of English church music, said that Elizabeth's reign "brought forth a noble birth, as of all learned men, so of Famous Composers in Church-Musick." That this is so true is a sign of the more settled and peaceful nature of the times: violent persecution was almost a thing of the past, and even staunch Catholics like Tallis, Byrd, Morley, and Tomkins were able to hold office in the Chapel Royal. The second Prayer Book, with all its vigorous denunciation of ceremonial, soon found itself faced with a

Latin translation, made by the Cambridge reformer Walter Haddon, and published in 1560. This Latin version of the Prayer Book was intended for use in the Universities, and in the colleges of Winchester and Eton, besides royal peculiars like St. George's Chapel, Windsor. Since Latin was allowed as the official language of the services—even of Holy Communion—it was an encouragement to composers to continue in their use of Latin texts. Even Protestant composers used Latin (usually Biblical) texts quite freely, with the result that it is extremely difficult to date a composer's output by the language employed, and even by the style of the music.

It is important that the Reformation in England should be visualized as a gradual change from the Sarum liturgy to the newly-established order of service in the English Church. The overlapping of artistic impulses and the lack of a clearly-defined liturgy over a long period caused a slow change in musical outlook, and that slow change was one of the greatest contributing factors to the continuity of tradition. Latin Masses were underlaid with an English text as early as 1545 by Taverner; on the other hand, new settings of the Mass were composed by Byrd during the last years of Elizabeth's reign, and were, though isolated, eventually published. A very great number of Elizabethan composers have left both Latin and English works, but it is not necessarily true that the former were written at an earlier point in the century than the latter. In the case of Tye, Tallis, John Munday, and Robert Parsons there is every reason to believe that the bulk of their Latin church music was written considerably later than their attempts to abide by Cranmerian formulas. The drive in favour of simplicity achieved a certain amount of purely musical good, however, and melismatic passages declined but did not entirely disappear. The resulting texture was refined without being exquisite, and freely contrapuntal without being dense and impenetrable. It was in this artistic milieu that Byrd came to learn music, and it was he whose technique and reputation (according to the loquacious commentator of a set of part-books in Christ Church, Oxford) was sufficient to free the English from Cicero's reproach of knowing nothing about music. It was Byrd who set for men's voices a short prayer for Queen Elizabeth: "O Lord, make thy servant Elizabeth our Queen to rejoice in thy strength; give her her heart's desire, and deny not the request of her lips, but prevent her with thine everlasting blessing, and give her a long life, even for ever and ever, Amen." By substituting names, the same anthem was used for James and even for Charles I.

Although the Elizabethan age saw the introduction of the verse anthem, in which certain sections are entrusted to solo voices, the principle is in fact very little different from that used in nearly all of the Marian motets of pre-Reformation times. They too had their sections intended for soloists alternating with the richer sonorities of the full choir. Again continuity is apparent; and the comparison is by no means weakened by the use of instruments for the accompaniment of verse anthems, for instruments too were used (though they are usually unspecified) in the Henrician motets. An Italian from Treviso, writing home his impressions of a Chapel Royal service in 1514, says: "after the procession High Mass commenced and was performed with great pomp, and with vocal and *instrumental* music, which lasted until 1 p.m."

This casual mention of the time of day serves to recall the tremendous differences in length between musical settings of the Ordinary of the Mass at the beginning and end of the century. A Fayrfax Mass consisting only of Gloria, Credo, Sanctus and Benedictus, and Agnus Dei takes nearly three-quarters of an hour to sing; yet each of Byrd's three Masses, which contain Kyries in addition, take roughly half that amount of time. The discrepancy is not due to any change or curtailment of Catholic ceremonial, but rather to a new musical outlook, in which aesthetic as well as liturgical considerations count for much.

On the whole, the middle years of Elizabeth's reign were a fairly safe haven for musicians: they could think and believe as they pleased, and they could write what pleased them. In setting the Communion service, they had to provide music for the Kyrie and Creed only; and for Morning and Evening Service the canticles were Venite, Te Deum, Benedictus, and Magnificat and Nunc Dimittis. Outside this framework, there was ample opportunity for the composition of anthems, or (if inspiration were lacking) for the adaptation of Latin motets to English words. Thus Taverner's technique of adaptation was revived, but for a reason different by far from that professed by its inventor.

THE ORDINARY OF
THE MASS

II

*T*HE HISTORY
of polyphonic settings of the Ordinary of
the Mass in Tudor days is both complex
and remarkable. Politico-religious disturb-
ances have caused the pattern of development to be less clear and orderly than it
might have been, since the Ordinary of the
Mass is looked upon as a relatively un-
changing liturgical entity, and one which
might well have engendered a uniform succession of English Masses conforming to
one type and style, in so far as the primary
characteristics of the form are concerned.
Those Masses which have come down to
us, either in their complete state or (as is
often the case) lacking one, two, or even
all but one voice-part, display an interest-

ing lack of uniformity which almost calls for a minute subdivision of every single type. The diversity of liturgical observance must have contributed greatly towards the conditions which produced their lack of uniformity, and it is not therefore surprising to find such diversity criticized in the Book of Common Prayer, where the Use of Salisbury, Hereford, Bangor, York, and Lincoln are once and for all time swept away—"now from henceforth all the whole realm shall have but one Use."

The Tudor Mass established itself upon the slenderest of traditions, and after rising to great musical heights suddenly vanished (as indeed it was bound to) until it reappeared under the stalwart, though circumspect aegis of William Byrd. In a period of less than fifty years, from the last decade of the fifteenth century until the troubled times when abbeys and monasteries were being despoiled to provide royal treasure, the Mass proved itself a vehicle for splendid and reverent musical adorn-

33

ment. In the hands of masters of the calibre of Dunstable, Power, and Benet, a similar reputation was built up in the early years of the fifteenth century; but between the death of Dunstable and the riper years of Fayrfax, Ludford, and Taverner there was very little to show in the field of integrated, cyclic settings of the Mass. This phenomenon, so common in insular sources, is reflected with great clarity in the seven choirbooks at Trent, which include less and less English music as the volumes progress. The earliest years of the Tudor dynasty apparently knew no other music for the Ordinary of the Mass than the modest three-voiced compositions of Walter Frye and Richard Cox, and the anonymous of the recently-discovered manuscript, now part of the Egerton collection in the British Museum. Frye's Mass, together with that of Cox, is preserved in a choirbook in the Royal Library of Brussels, and although both works may have been written on the continent, they exhibit certain English characteristics which stamp them as being well apart from the main stream of Franco-Flemish sacred polyphony. They both make use of the Kyrie trope *Deus creator omnium,* the presence of which in Dufay's *Caput* Mass has given rise to the suggestion that even Dufay may have based his composition on an English model. *Deus creator omnium* is an important Sarum trope, the one designated for all Principal Doubles—the Feasts of the Nativity, the Epiphany, Easter Day, Ascension Day, Whitsun Day, the Assumption, the Anniversary of the Place, and the Dedication of a Church.

The widespread fame of this Kyrie trope is demonstrated by its occurrence in an organ Mass by a Welsh composer, Philip ap Rhys, and in a four-part Mass by the Scot, Robert Carver. Both use not only the verbal text (as Frye and Cox did), but also the proper chant for the trope, as a cantus firmus. Nevertheless, it is true to say that the polyphonic Kyrie never be-

came fashionable in England, and consequently most insular Masses begin with
[*Gloria in excelsis Deo*] *et in terra pax.*
The reason for the omission of the Kyrie
is bound up with liturgical practice and
the demands of ceremonial customs, as
well as the availability of a rich and varied
repertoire of tropes. It so happened that
the Kyrie occurred when there was a
momentary lull in the ceremonies at High
Mass: the priest, preceded by his ministers
and acolytes, approached the altar to the
singing of the Introit and Psalm, and after
the Introit had been repeated, *Gloria Patri*
was sung. Then followed the Confession,
Absolution, the Kiss of Peace, the bringing of bread and wine and water for the
Eucharist, and the blessing of incense. The
Introit was repeated for the third and last
time, and the Kyrie followed. During the
singing of Introit and Kyrie, the priest and
his ministers were to sit in the sedilia and
wait until the choir finished. Even plainsong for Introit and Kyrie would take up

two or three minutes, a ninefold polyphonic Kyrie about ten minutes. This was clearly far too long a time to have to wait, and accordingly harmonized settings of Kyrie were discouraged. It is noticeable, however, that as the sixteenth century progressed, composers began to write *alternatim* Kyries as a kind of compromise. A typical example, by Christopher Tye, provides polyphony for the second, fourth, sixth, and eighth invocations, the remaining five being sung to the implied plainchant, which is *Orbis factor*. Tye does not use the text of the trope—only the melody, and that in a highly elaborated form. The two Kyrie invocations are for four voices, while the intervening sections set to *Christe eleison* are given to a duo and a trio respectively. The complete Kyrie would require four or five minutes in performance, and would thus appear to satisfy both aesthetic and practical demands. William Munday, Hyett, Shepherd, and Taverner were among the other composers who compromised in the same way as Tye did.

Among the very few Masses containing a Kyrie are *Surrexit pastor bonus* (Lupus Italus), the *Mass for a Meane* (Appleby), and the Masses by William Munday and William Byrd. The remaining four sections, Gloria, Credo, Sanctus, and Agnus Dei, are found in practically every Tudor Mass, and this was regarded as a standard grouping in much the same way as the four-movement symphony was to become an accepted form of more recent times. Single Mass-sections are found occasionally, and they usually imply the loss of the other three members, rather than their suppression. Such is the case with a Kyrie and Gloria by Turges, a composer of the early years of the sixteenth century. It is highly unlikely that these two sections form a Mass-pair on the lines of the well-known fifteenth century practice, which in any case shows preference for pairs of Gloria-Credo and Sanctus-Agnus. It was the custom for most polyphonic settings of Gloria and Credo to begin at *et in terra pax* and *Patrem omnipotentem* respectively, the intonations being sung by the celebrant. There are, however certain divergences from this practice. Both of Munday's Masses *Upon the Square* begin the Credo at *factorem caeli;* so too does the four-part Mass *Pater creator omnium* by Robert Carver. The works by Munday also contain slightly different schemes for Sanctus and Agnus, which it was the custom to set complete. The first *Sanctus* is intoned, and Munday begins his polyphonic setting at *Sanctus, Sanctus Dominus Deus Sabaoth*. Similarly, the first *Agnus Dei* is intoned, in accordance with strict liturgical custom.

The treatment of the text of *Credo in unum Deum* in the majority of Tudor Masses would appear to be somewhat less strict, for omission of certain phrases was frequent and by no means confined to one composer or one period. The latter part of the Credo, from *et resurrexit tertia die* to the end, is the usual place for omissions, although John Shepherd, in his Masses *Be not afraid, The Western Wynde* and *The French Mass,* omits the phrase *Deum de Deo . . . de Deo vero.* Indeed, his treatment of the texts is extraordinarily unorthodox, for he even omits phrases from the Gloria. There are at least ten different Credo omissions, some long and some short, but it is significant to note that composers do not adhere to any single pattern of omission. Taverner and Ludford, for example, use three each, and Ludford is noteworthy (along with Munday, Rasar, Lupus Italus, and Whitbrooke) for setting the entire text without any omissions. It has been shown that the troped polyphonic Kyrie was discouraged owing to the amount of time taken to sing it, and a similar conclusion must be reached after considering the many conflicting explanations for omitting clauses in the Credo. Political and religious arguments may at times have affected the structure of the liturgy, even to the extent

of altering texts of great sanctity and significance, but as far as the Tudor Mass is concerned it is clear that the Credo omissions
were made for the sake of time. The melismatic style which was so much to the
fore in Henrician times did much to prevent composers from compressing texts into
a small musical space. In Taverner's Mass
Corona spinea, two treble voices sing florid
passages on one vowel ("o" of *Domini,* in
the Benedictus) for the space of one minute, before changing to the next syllable.
This example is far from being excep-
tional: it is a common manifestation of
a latter-day "jubilus" technique which
the English inherited from fifteenth-century continental composers. This technique, which was in direct opposition to
the *parlando* style prevalent in the four-
teenth century England, was bound to
elongate even a normal text of relatively
short length. Since the Credo has the long-
est text of the sung portions of the Ordinary, it had to be curtailed in order to

41

match the other sections. In this connection it is interesting to note that composers often went to some trouble to make the four sections of the polyphonic Mass fairly equal in length, so that a Mass section by Fayrfax, Taverner, Ludford, and their contemporaries lasts about nine or ten minutes.

A less frequently found, but none the less important, feature of style in the Tudor Mass is the *alternatim* scheme, whose importance in the music for the Choir Office has already been emphasized. That it has its place in the Ordinary of the Mass has already been seen in the description of the isolated Kyrie settings by Tye and others. Tye, incidentally, may have carried the principles of alteration between chant and polyphony into the realm of the Proper, for he has left harmonized versions of certain interior strophes of the Sequence *Post partum virgo*. The remaining strophes may originally have existed as polyphonic music for a larger number of voice-parts than the two small sections preserved, for it was the

42

custom to collect three- and four-part sections of larger works for performance as vocal chamber music in the home. Until further evidence becomes available, however, it must be conceded that the *alternatim* scheme has a strong claim, especially since there is corroborative evidence in the Sequence *Fulgens praeclara,* composed by Thomas Preston for organ and plainchant.

Continental p r a c t i c e corresponds in main outlines to English practice where alternation is concerned, and there is a further link in the fact that its use is comparatively infrequent. A Gloria by Dufay, the *Missa Paschalis* of Isaak, and the Mantuan Masses by Palestrina are the most celebrated continental works in this genre. In England, there are the seven Masses by Ludford, Shepherd's *Mass for a Meane,* and two of the York Masses, which form far more convincing Gloria-Credo pairs than the two sections of a Mass by Turges mentioned previously. The Masses by Ludford are all for three voices, and are

43

preserved in three part-books. A fourth book contains those parts of the Ordinary destined to be sung—or even played by an elaborating organist—alternately with the polyphony. Ludford shows much contrapuntal felicity in managing three-voiced texture; yet in doing so he seems to be looking back rather than forward, echoing as it were the sparse and solemn sounds of the fifteenth century, of *Rex seculorum, Gruene Linden,* and *O rosa bella.*

Shepherd, in contrast to Ludford (who sets all the movements in *alternatim* style) has only the Gloria and Credo broken up in this way. Once again there is divergence as to what phrases are given to polyphonists, and what to the singers of plainchant, just in the same way as there was divergence in the length and location of Credo omissions. Turning now to the York Masses, it is interesting to compare the one alternating Kyrie with those previously discussed, for the scheme is exactly the same: invocations 2, 4, 6, and 8 are set for choir,

and the remaining ones are to be chanted.
The composer is William Horwood, two of
whose compositions survive complete in the
Eton choirbook. The first of the two short
alternatim Masses (both are anonymous)
has a slightly retrospective air, with complex and inconsistent notation giving more
than a hint of some late Plantagenet ama-
teur. The second Mass is, by contrast, very
straightforward from a notational point of
view, and makes considerable use of imitative patterns and smoothly-flowing counterpoint. This Mass is based upon a short
versicle *Custodi nos, Domine,* sung immediately after the hymn at Compline, and
here provided with a decorative cauda. In
the Gloria the predominant texture is four-
part, and cadences use the total number of
voices for every verse. But the layout of the
Credo is more elaborate: after two four-
part verses there comes a duo for treble
and bass (*Et incarnatus*) followed by a trio
for *Et ascendit.* The remaining verses are
full.

A noteworthy insular feature of Tudor Masses is the range of texture and the choice of voice-parts. There are no Masses extant for less than three voices or more than ten, and the credit for spanning this wide range goes to the Scottish composer Robert Carver. He wrote Masses for three, four, five, six, and ten voices. The usual choice of Tudor composers was for five voices ranging from treble to bass, but occasionally special circumstances called for unusual resources, and the result was that a small number of works are set "for a meane," that is for a counter-tenor, whose part is usually the highest of four. Two Masses by Thomas Appleby and John Shepherd have this title in the manuscript sources which have come down to us; other works, however, have equal claim to the title, since their highest part is comfortably within alto range. Tallis's four-part Mass is an obvious and readily available example, and another (this time five-part) Mass equally suitable for men's voices is

Sine nomine by John Taverner. Masses of this type were undoubtedly very useful when the choirboys were away on holiday, the men being left to sing the polyphonic parts of the service on their own.

In considering the wide variety of types which exists in the Tudor Mass, it is important to realize that a very great number of Masses rely on a cantus firmus, whose normal position is in the tenor part. The cantus firmus, when liturgical, gave the work its *raison d'être,* since the feast for which the Mass was intended was usually represented by an antiphon or respond from the Office of the day. The plainchant thus chosen would be elongated, and possibly broken up, in order to form a definite mensural scheme. If the plainsong were long, as in the antiphon *O quam suavis* used for the Mass of that name, it would not appear very often in its complete form. In fact it appears only twice in this particular Mass, which recent research has shown to be very probably the work of

John Lloyd. A shorter plainsong, such as *Corona spinea,* appears ten times during the course of Taverner's Mass for the Feast of the Crown of our Lord. The composer was thus free in the first instance to choose a plainsong which would serve as a scaffold for his polyphony, but having once chosen it, he would be bound by its length to a greater or lesser number of repetitions. The normal practice was to allow the cantus firmus to appear only during the sections for full choir. Other sections in duo or trio would make use of independent motives. There were, of course, many exceptions to this general rule, since Tudor composers followed the dictates of their own musical conscience rather than a set formula or method of composition. As an additional piece of unifying structural aid, composers nearly always made use of a short phrase common to the beginnings of all four sections of the Mass. It has become the custom in recent years to call this a head-motive, a term derived from the German *Kopf-*

motiv. This term is quite suitable provided it is clearly understood that the motive is not merely a melodic tag: it is a polyphonic segment, and recurs as such at the beginning of Gloria, Credo, Sanctus, and Agnus Dei. Most Tudor composers appear to have used it instinctively, though by no means indiscriminately. Fayrfax, for example, uses a head-motive for his Mass *Tecum principium,* but the separate voice-parts of the motive are gradually decorated as the Mass proceeds, so that when Agnus Dei is reached the motive as such is hardly recognizable.

Among the many Masses conforming to this type, which combines cantus firmus and head-motive, are those of Alwood, Ashwell, Jones, Knight, Ludford, Lloyd, Lupus, Aston, Fayrfax, Taverner, and Carver. The cantus firmus of Alwood's Mass consists of only five notes, which are repeated in varying rhythmical combinations, the final *dona nobis pacem* being moulded upon a quintuple scheme. The title

49

of the Mass *Praise Him Praiseworthy* may have been derived from a para-liturgical source, for the five syllables fit the five notes of the theme and may originally have been associated with it. Ashwell's Mass *Ave Maria* draws upon the plainchant of the antiphon of the same name, and contains a rare example of double gymell in the Gloria, where trebles and altos are both divided at one point, giving a complete and rich harmonic effect of high tessitura. This treatment of the phrase *qui tollis peccata mundi* is also to be found at the same place in another Mass by the same composer, based this time upon a short respond for Prime in Easter Week, *Jesu Christe*. Dunstable's Mass *Jesu Christe* is, incidentally, indebted to a cognate plainsong, though the source is slightly different, and is used only in Ascensiontide. The Masses by Jones (*Spes noster*), Knight (*Libera nos*), and Lupus (*Surrexit pastor bonus*) are unfortunately defective, owing to missing part-books, but they certainly owe their titles to plainchant cantus firmi. Ludford, in his Mass for the Feast of the Annunciation (*Christi Virgo*) indulges in brilliant and florid part-writing which must have taxed the powers of his singers very severely. A more sober, though none the less brilliant testimony of his powers as a contrapuntist is the Mass *Videte miraculum,* which makes use of the respond so named for the Feast of the Purification.

Other Masses by Ludford belong to this type, as well as all the known Masses of Robert Fayrfax, who was his greatest contemporary. Fayrfax has long been noted for his fluid, luminous counterpoint, which seems to combine the virtues of the late fifteenth-century school with the newly-found powers of a younger generation. He must have had access to earlier sources, and certainly knew Dunstable's motet *Albanus roseo,* for the beautiful but recondite theme used in this motet appears in his Mass *Albanus*, and is there subjected to a remarkable treatment involving total inversion and retrograde movement. The theme is taken from an antiphon which appears in a rhymed office for St. Alban. Two other Masses, *Regali* and *Tecum principium,* are built upon antiphons, for the Conception of the B.V.M. and for the Feast of the Nativity respectively. The treatment of the head-motive in the latter work has already been discussed; in the former, it is normal and regular.

Taverner came as a worthy successor to Fayrfax, and inherited many of the earlier master's technical traits. There is little in the way of padding in his gracious and limpid melismata: each phrase is imbued with a life of its own, each sequence has an artistic climax and a graceful cadence. The most important of his cantus firmus Masses are *Corona spinea, O Michael,* and *Gloria tibi Trinitas.* The first of these has already been mentioned in connection with Taverner's vocal style; it is a work on the largest possible scale, and suggests that the

Feast of the Crown on our Lord, although added at a fairly late stage in the Sarum Kalendar, was held in special esteem at Tattershall or Oxford, where Taverner spent most of his working life. The Mass *O Michael* is not, as its name suggests, for the principal feast of St. Michael on September 29; the cantus firmus (most unusually) has a different incipit from the title of the Mass. It is the respond *Archangeli Michaelis,* sung at procession on the Feast of St. Michael in Monte Tumba, which took place on October 16. The "O" in the title of the Mass may therefore stand for October: it is certainly not an invocation. *Gloria tibi Trinitas* takes its name from an antiphon sung at Second Vespers on Trinity Sunday, and it has achieved recent fame through being exposed as the unwitting progenitor of a century and a half of English chamber music: the "In nomine" compositions which lasted until the time of Purcell were nearly all based upon the same antiphon, as it appeared in the *in nomine Domini* section of Taverner's Benedictus.

It would be tempting to continue this survey of the mainstream of Mass settings in Tudor times, but there are certain tributaries which demand attention, and they are still, almost inevitably, connected with the cantus firmus principle. An important group in its own right is the small number of works based on a secular or paraliturgical cantus firmus. English composers showed no enthusiasm similar to that of their continental contemporaries when it was a question of bringing in a secular tune. There is, for example, only one example of a Mass on *L'homme armé*—that by Robert Carver—although dozens exist in Europe. Shepherd, Taverner, and Tye all wrote four-part Masses on *The Western Wynde,* and it has been said that Carver too based his three-part Mass on this secular song. The first few notes of the theme do, in fact, occur in the treble part of Carver's Mass, but the resemblance goes no further than this, and seems to be purely coincidental. Tye's Mass, on the other hand, gives the complete theme to the altos throughout the work, and they sing it no less than twenty-nine times. This feat of endurance may have been intended as a musical riposte to Taverner, who gives the tune to all the voices in turn except the altos. A secular origin may also be assumed for the theme of Taverner's Mass *Small Devotion* (not *in all Devotion,* as some contend). Titles such as Shepherd's *Be not afraid* may have come from the Bible, though there may be no real liturgical significance, any more than in the same composer's *French Mass,* whose title simply refers to the style in which the music was composed. The so-called Playnsong Masses by Shepherd and Taverner are, by a queer twist of irony, not based on plainsong at all: they rely upon a simple (or plain) chordal counterpoint, with very little elaboration. Burton's Mass *Ut re mi fa sol la* speaks for itself: the hexachord theme,

55

beginning on f, rises to d and then falls again to f. The Masses *Upon the Square* by Munday and Whitbroke have been variously and ingeniously explained: the true explanation, however, is bound up with square notation. Certain models in cantus fractus were used by these two composers (and by the anonymous composer of two Kyries in John Baldwin's manuscript) and more or less decorated according to the needs of the music. These "square" sources go back to the early fifteenth century, and provided another link between the schools of Dunstable and Fayrfax.

Few examples of *contrafacta* or parody Masses have so far been discovered in England: this technique, like that of using a secular cantus firmus, had apparently not gained a firm footing in Tudor England. The first authenticated example of a parody Mass is usually thought to be *O bone Jesu,* which Fayrfax based upon a motet (similarly named) of his own composition. Only one voice-part of the motet survives, but it is enough to show the link between the two works. Later parodies survive in Taverner's Mass *Small Devotion* (based on his motet *Christi Jesu pastor bone*) and the Mass and motet on *Salve intemerata virgo* by Tallis.

The very small category of Masses without cantus firmus contain three of the most famous settings of all: the Masses for three, four, and five voices by Byrd. These were probably written towards the end of Elizabeth's reign, and were published early in the reign of James I. A copy of the three-part Mass in Baldwin's manuscript follows a piece dated 1603; this may refer merely to the date of copying, and not of composition. All three Masses make use of a head-motive, although this use is irregular. One motive appears in all incipits of the three-part Mass, except the Sanctus. Two motives are used for the Mass *a 4*, Credo alone being unaffected, while the Mass *a 5* has a similar arrangement of paired motives, in which the Sanctus is once again formed of separate melodic material. Each Mass has a Kyrie. Tallis's four-part Mass also uses head-motives, and is almost unique in being a parody upon itself, since all the sections of the Gloria from *propter magnam gloriam tuam* onwards appear in the succeeding sections, with only very small and insignificant changes. Carver's Masses *a 3* and *a 6* lack cantus firmus but are unified by head-motives, and the same is true of Taverner's *Sine nomine* and *Small Devotion* Masses, besides the fine six-part Mass *Euge bone* by Christopher Tye.

THE MOTET

III

*T*HE TERM "MO-
tet" is generally employed in contradistinc-
tion to the term "anthem"; yet at one time
chronology appears to have been tempor-
arily reversed, and the latter word (variously spelled as "antemne," "antempe,"
and so forth) made to refer to what would
now be called a motet. It is somewhat un-
fortunate that this all-embracing word has
been used, for the past century or so, in a
loose and misleading manner; so that, by
a process which is literally a reduction to
the absurd, all polyphonic vocal music
which is not part of the Ordinary of the
Mass has been dubbed "motet." A similar
confusion exists in sixteenth century title
pages and inventories, although this is no
excuse for the perpetuation in modern

59

editions of so ill-defined an attitude. Even the august and scholarly volumes of *Tudor Church Music* perpetuate this confusing situation, where very little is done to show the liturgical background to the wide variety of works represented. Antiphons, responds, hymns, sequences, and many other important liturgical forms are carelessly classed with large-scale extra-liturgical compositions (usually in honour of the Virgin) as "motets," which some of them are not, and never could have been. The true and only criterion is, of course, the verbal text: if this is found in antiphoners and breviaries, a liturgical occasion can be assigned to the work in question. If not, then the music almost certainly belongs to some occasion no less devout, but nevertheless outside the actual liturgy.

The hymns and psalms of the daily office, or canonical hours of prayer, were usually sung to the appointed plainchants. Polyphonic music entered the ceremonies rarely, except during Matins, Vespers, and

Compline. At Matins, it was the hymn *Te Deum* which was most frequently set in polyphony; at Vespers, *Magnificat* held pride of place. But it was after Compline (sometimes even after Vespers) that the most elaborate musical offering of the day was made—an antiphon, set in the most resplendent and sonorous polyphony, was sung in honour of the Virgin. The Sarum form of Compline contained none of the four antiphons to the B.V.M. which have always been an important part of this service in the Roman rite. The singing of these antiphons was, however, frequently prescribed by special statutes of colleges, guilds, and cathedrals, either as part of the Hours of the Blessed Virgin, or as an evening devotion to her. The statutes for Henry VI's foundations of King's College Cambridge and Eton College prescribe the singing of an antiphon every evening; in the case of Eton the title of the antiphon for Lent—*Salve regina*—appears in the statute itself. Outside Lent, any other antiphon in honour of the Virgin was allowed to be sung. *Salve regina* was also prescribed in Thomas Elys's foundation deed for the chantry of St. Thomas the Martyr at Sandwich, and as a matter of course in the statutes of the chantry established in the church of St. Magnus, London Bridge, where there existed a guild "de Salve Regina" from the reign of Edward III.

In the earliest and perhaps the greatest collection of early Tudor motets, the Eton choirbook, there were sixteen settings of *Salve regina,* ranging from five to nine voice-parts. The next most frequently-set text was *Gaude flore virginali,.* a hymn in commemoration of the Five Joys of the B.V.M. The first word of this hymn came to denote the candles, or "gawdyes," which were lit before the image of the Virgin during the singing of the antiphon. Other hymns to the Virgin in the Eton choirbook are *Gaude virgo mater Christi* (three settings, with a fourth which diverges after the incipit into a different poem), *Gaude*

virgo salutata, O regina celestis gloriae,
and *Stella celi* (a hymn against the plague,
beseeching the Virgin for divine protection). The style of these Marian motets—
for they are motets in the proper sense of
the word—is noble and pious, yet full of
contrast and complexity. *Salve regina* is
troped (that is, provided with extra verses,
usually sung by soloists) in many of the
early Tudor settings: Browne, Cornysch,
Davy, Fayrfax, Hacomplaynt, Hampton,
Howchyn, Hygons, Lambe, Ludford, Sutton, and Wylkynson are among the many
composers who used the troped version of
the antiphon, the performance of which
must have lasted nearly a quarter of an
hour. Some of the settings are based on
cantus firmi taken from the office of Feasts
of the B.V.M., or from other important
liturgical occasions: the compositions by
Browne and Hygons can both be connected
with Maundy Thursday, while Sutton's
seven-part setting is based on an antiphon
for Trinity Sunday.

As soon as a text became reasonably standardized, it became the fashion to change certain features while yet relating the sense and sentiment to the adoration of the Virgin. Ludford, for example, has set the text *Salve regina pudica mater,* and Fawkyner the text *Salve regina vas mundicie.* Similar changes were wrought upon *Ave Maria,* which in the hands of Arthur Chamberlayne became *Ave gratia plena Maria tecum Dominus* . . . . . . and in John Mason's setting *Ave fuit prima salus* . . . . *Maria dum salutaris* . . . . *Gracia sanctispiritus* . . . . *Plena tu es virtutibus.* Each word of the antiphon became the initial word of a short sentence, and each of these sentences is separated by an acclamation *Ave Maria,* so that the final effect is that of a trope within a trope. Tallis, in his magnificent *Ave rosa sine spinis,* has troped the antiphon in such a way as to transform it into a Marian motet of almost symphonic proportions. Thus, nearly all of the motets in honour of the Virgin are extended in length besides being extensive, and they are set out for five or more voice-parts in the richest possible polyphony. A very great number of different texts was used; some being metrical hymns, others sequences or proses. The presence of a cantus firmus was felt to be less and less obligatory as the century wore on, so that compositions similar in all other respects to the earlier types no longer anchored themselves to plainchant: Johnson's *Gaude Maria virgo,* Carver's *Gaude flore virginali,* and Tallis's *Salve intemerata virgo* are all examples of this newer style of composition. Yet at the other end of the scale stands Lambe's *O regina celestis glorie,* which is built upon two distinct cantus firmi sung simultaneously. Its structural layout and high degree of technical competence recall a work written only a decade or so later—the motet *Optime pastor* which Isaak wrote for the accession of Pope Leo X.

Worship of the Virgin inspired not only a large number of settings of *Magnificat,* but even affected *Te Deum,* which was sometimes given the paraphrastic text *Te matrem Dei laudamus,* Aston's work being the best known and most readily accessible. *Magnificat,* on the other hand, was held to be one of the most sacred of all sacred texts, and was never troped or altered in any way. It was almost invariably composed for alternating plainsong and polyphony, and since the plainsong for the canticle was so well-known, the custom was to give only the polyphonic verses, which began *et exultavit.* The great choirbooks of Eton, Caius, Lambeth, and Edinburgh are rich in settings of *Magnificat,* and significantly enough the part-books of the mid-sixteenth century are correspondingly poor due to the gradual suppression of Mariolatry by Cranmer and the reformers. In its finest and most imposing settings, the canticle of the Virgin was almost like a personal offering or prayer of the composer himself, and no composer of the Henrician period, whether famous or humble, neglected to write a *Magnificat*. It was a solemn duty, and the result was often a solemn and impressive polyphonic canvas, set off by a framework of plainsong verses which served both to heighten contrast and to give relief to the ear. The examples by Fayrfax, Ludford, Cornysch, Appleby, and Jones all display a sure yet flexible technique, and in spite of their strength and solidity they contain gracious melodic lines and sensitive counterpoint. They rarely use the tone (to which the odd-numbered verses are set) as a cantus firmus throughout the entire work, though occasionally it appears in the opening verse and at the end. Appleby and Darke use this method, while Ludford and others prefer to hint at the tone by means of strong melodic progressions in the tenor part. Byrd has left us no Latin setting of *Magnificat,* although there are two from the pen of his teacher, Thomas Tallis, and fine examples by the elder Munday, and by Shepherd and Taverner.

The principle of alternation was applied generously to hymn-tunes, and to a lesser extent to psalms. Hymns for Matins, Vespers, and Compline, normally sung to plainchant, were divided between the choir and the assembled priests or monks in such a way that the first verse and remaining odd-numbered verses were chanted, and the even verses sung in polyphony. A rubric from the Erlyngham Breviary shows that this principle of alternation was built upon a hallowed liturgical practice of great antiquity: "The ruler of the choir should begin the hymn as far as the second or third word; and the choir on the side of the officiating priest continue that verse, and the other part of the choir on the other side, the next verse; and so they alternate each verse to the end; which is to be observed throughout the whole year; the choir at the end of the last verse responding *Amen*." In the Sarum ritual, the ruler of the choir was a priest who acted as a liaison between precentor and choir. It was his duty to enquire the antiphon on the psalms, and the intonation of the psalm, from the Precentor; and similarly to supervise the participation in hymns, canticles, and responsories.

In the same way that *Magnificat* was referred to by the opening words of its second verse *et exultavit,* so the hymns were listed by their second verse—a fact which has caused them to be re-edited and even published and recorded in a misleading form. Thus *Hic nempe mundi gaudia* is not a motet by Tallis, but a set of polyphonic verses for five-part choir, based on the plainchant hymn *Deus tuorum militium.* According to the rubric just quoted, the hymn would be sung as follows:

Ruler   : Deus tuorum militum

Cantors : Sors et corona, praemium: } plain-
            Laudes canentes Martyris, } chant
            Absolve nexu criminis.

Choir   : Hic nempe mundi gaudia . . polyphony

Cantors : Poenas cucurrit fortiter . . . plainchant

Choir   : Ob hoc precatu supplici . .polyphony
Cantors : Deo Patri sit gloria . . . . .plainchant

Amen would probably have been sung by all present, but when the last verse happened to be set polyphonically, the *Amen* was often harmonized too. Shepherd and Tallis have both left settings of *Deus tuorum militum,* also of *Salvator mundi Domine, Jam Christus astra ascenderat,* and *Jesu salvator seculi.* There are seven more alternatim hymns from the pen of John Shepherd, and three different ones besides these from Thomas Tallis. The latter shows a tendency towards economy of form by setting verse 4 of *Sermone blando angelus* to the same music as verse 2, and similarly verse 8 to the music of verse 6. A decline in the popularity of cantus firmus verses and alternatim performance came about in the time of William Munday and Byrd, probably after 1570, although a fine setting by Munday of *A solis ortus cardine* is extant. Byrd composed alternatim versions of *Sacris sollemniis* and *Pange lingua,* although his most famous hymn is a through-composed setting of *Christe qui lux es,* in which the tune (sung in plainchant for the first verse only) is given to each of the five voices in turn for the remainder of the hymn.

His alternatim hymns demonstrate with admirable clarity two entirely different methods of setting the chant: in *Sacris sollemniis* the three polyphonic verses keep the melody in the highest part, and always in even note-values. The other four parts are based on imitative figures which are melodically independent of the chant itself, except in the last verse, where they are indebted to the opening phrase. The plainchant of *Pange lingua,* on the other hand, is placed not at the top where it can be heard, but right in the middle of the texture, and even there it is further obscured by an extremely free treatment of the melodic line. White, in his *Christe qui lux es,* has a regular cantus firmus in the tenor, a voice which is rarely favoured in Tallis's hymns. Tallis prefers to entrust the melody to the highest voice, and his usual method is to decorate the melody slightly, often in compound duple rhythm, for the opening verses; and then to present it in even note-values and sober guise for the last verse.

Polyphonic psalm settings appear much more rarely than hymns during the early Tudor period, although notable exceptions show that similar technical processes were applied to complete psalms for important feasts. Experiments began in the reign of Henry VII with the erasure of alternate plainsong verses in liturgical books such as processionals and antiphoners, and the substitution of mensural notation for the chant. In one instance it has been possible to reconstruct an alternatim faburden scheme for the psalms *Laudate Dominum* and *In exitu Israel,* sung during the procession to the font at Vespers on Easter Day. The same psalms have been set jointly by Shepherd, Byrd, and W. Munday, and as all three were members of the Chapel Royal together it is quite possible that they may have collaborated in this way.

Texts from the Bible, and especially from the Psalms, replaced the Marian hymns and sequences which had been so popular with composers of the Fayrfax period. The non-liturgical and therefore motet style of these compositions is often proved by the fact that a few verses only are set, and sometimes these are neither consecutive nor alternate, but simply selections from a psalm with a view to making up a text of a certain length and in a certain mood. No doxology was sung, though some of the settings end with a polyphonic Amen. Motets of this type rarely use a cantus firmus; their texture is a closely integrated mesh of imitative melodic fragments, worked out with considerable skill and a high regard for individual voice-progressions. The examples by Tallis, W. Munday, Byrd, Parsons, and Shepherd are typical and illustrative of the new motet style of the Elizabethan period. Not only are the words of the text allowed to influence the music in a direct manner, whenever this is desirable and effective—they are even permitted a more Humanistic function in stressing the composer's own feelings. Although examples of this extremely subjective treatment are rare, they are quite unmistakable when seen in the context of a normal psalm verse. W. Munday's *Memor esto verbi tui* breaks forth into double gymell at the words *Cantabiles mihi erant justificationes tuae;* and his son John Munday, in a setting of *In te Domine speravi,* uses exactly the same technique— incidentally enlarging the texture to seven real parts—at the words *Vide humilitatem meam et laborem meum.* For sheer musical labour it would be difficult to better Tallis's *Spem in alium,* written in forty parts (for eight five-part choirs) and a musical monument of impressive sound and proportions. Nevertheless, Tallis was not unique in having produced so vast a canvas, for Italian and Spanish composers of the sixteenth century exerted their contrapuntal ingenuity to similar ends.

Tallis and Byrd together composed and published the first collection of Latin motets ever to be printed in England— *Cantiones quae ab argumento Sacrae vocantur* (1575). The acceptance by Queen Elizabeth of the dedication of this work is not surprising in view of her support of the Latin Prayer Book, and her approval of services in Latin on special occasions and in special places. The texts set by Byrd and Tallis are in any case non-controversial in that they contain nothing written in honour of the Virgin, but they are far from being non-liturgical, in spite of the number of settings in motet-style of psalm verses and Biblical texts. There are several hymns, a few settings of short antiphons (*Miserere mihi, Domine* by Byrd, and two settings of *Salvator mundi salva nos,* for Holy Cross Day, by Tallis) and several polyphonic elaborations of responsorial chant. Byrd's *Libera me,* with its two related sections, must alternate with plainchant, as must the short respond *Candidi facti sunt Nazarei,* composed by Tallis. A polyphonic responsory of greater stature is the same composer's *Honor virtus et potestas,* for Trinity Sunday.

In 1589 and 1591, Byrd, this time alone, published his two books of *Cantiones Sacrae.* Like the earlier collection, these were retrospective publications, containing works which had for years been circulated in manuscript copies, often defective and unreliable. The two books of *Gradualia* (1605 and 1607) may well have been composed in the last years of Elizabeth's reign, and it is therefore possible to consider them as part of, if not the very summit, of our musical heritage from Tudor England. For although Byrd lived on until 1623, his training, technique, and outlook were nothing if not Elizabethan, and his music shows clearly how slowly and yet how relentlessly he moved towards his ideal conception of the link between tonal art and liturgical function. He knew that perfection in vocal music came only when it was "framed to the life of the words"—an expression which he used in his *Psalms, Songs, and Sonnets* of 1611. The two books of *Cantiones Sacrae* demonstrate the great decline of the cantus firmus motet, of which there are only two examples (*Aspice Domine* in book I, and *Descendit de coelis* in book II) the remainder of the words being unified by an expressive and imitative style of composition quite independent of plainsong influences. The *Gradualia,* whose two books constitute a great liturgical rarity—settings of the Proper of Feasts of the Virgin, and of Corpus Christi, All Saints, Christmas, Epiphany, Easter, and Whitsun, together with the Feast of the Ascension and that of St. Peter and St. Paul—embody techniques which are even more restrained and refined, bearing out in musical sounds the thought which Byrd had expressed in his long dedication to Lord Northampton. The part played by the texts in the inspiration of the music is rightly thrown into relief by Byrd, who found that meditation on the words often caused the themes to suggest themselves spontaneously. In most instances the inspiration seems to have been of a general nature, reflecting the mood and sense of the text in so far as that is possible; yet on occasion Byrd has allowed himself to be affected by the word rather than by the phrase, and accordingly he describes the word in terms of pure music. These effects, seldom but always tastefully used, are for the ear rather than for the eye; they constitute word-sounding, not word-painting.

Music was often composed in Tudor times for special services and state occasions, and some of the motets belonging to this class have already been discussed. Para-liturgical motets are much more rare, for they do not form part of the liturgy, nor do their texts come from the Bible. For this reason the texts and the musical settings vary much more than other more strictly liturgical genres. *O bone Jesu,* which was set by Robert Carver, Robert Fayrfax, Robert Parsons, and one anonymous composer, illustrates the difference in length and internal structure due to differences of textual disposition. The prayer consists fundamentally of a number of short petitions separated by acclamations similar to those which appear in *Salve regina.* The anonymous setting begins *O bone Jesu, O dulcis Jesu, O mitis Jesu;* Carver and Fayrfax diverge after the opening words to a series of superlatives—*O piissime Jesu, O dulcissime Jesu.* Fayrfax and anonymous agree about the ending, but Carver is far more extended, and instead of finishing with *Amen* he adds several more petitions and another group of superlative acclamations: a fitting conclusion for a motet in nineteen real parts. The motet by Parsons is different entirely, for it makes use of a framework of psalm verses with interpolated acclamations such as *O Adonay, O Heloy, O Emmanuel, O Raby.*

Polyphonic settings of the Lamentations of Jeremiah varied only in the number of lessons composed: the structure was basically the same, and included harmonizations of the Hebrew letters preceding each section. Fragments exist by John Munday and Ferrabosco, while there are more complete settings by White and Tallis. It was intended for male voices only, and the dark tone colour which results is entirely in keeping with the penitential character of the text. Both of White's settings call for boys' voices, and achieve their solemnity and dignity more from the innate reverence of the counterpoint than from any unusual textural feature. Of two noteworthy polyphonic versions of the Passion according to St. Matthew, one is anonymous, and was probably composed before the end of Henry VIII's reign, while the other (also for four voices) is earlier still. It is preserved in the Eton choirbook, and is unfortunately one of the incomplete works; but enough remains to show the skill and resources of its author, Richard Davy, who was at one time organist of Magdalen College, Oxford. He is the composer who is said to have written *O domine celi terreque* in one day. If this statement, found in the Eton choirbook, is true, then Davy must have been endowed with a quick brain as well as great contrapuntal skill, for the work in question is scored for five-part choir and lasts about seventeen minutes.

A comparison of his motet *In honore summae Matris* with one by Byrd, *Non vos relinquam orphanos,* displays the great differences in style caused by the century of change and development which separated them. Davy's motet is in the Eton choirbook: Byrd's is taken from the second book of *Gradualia.* Both are five-part settings, and both have exactly the same overall vocal range—22 notes, as the Eton designation expresses it. But there the resemblance ends. Discounting the obvious physical differences between a setting of a lengthy hymn to the Virgin and a relatively short polyphonic antiphon to the *Magnificat,* the contrasts of style are quite remarkable.

Davy evolves an ever-changing plan of remarkable complexity which serves purposes both useful and artistic. The greater part of his composition consists of duos and trios for various combinations of solo voices, not necessarily adjacent. Indeed, there are several instances of fairly long sections for soprano and tenor, or even soprano and bass, and it so happens that both of these duo-combinations (so often found in pre-Reformation vocal music) sound as effective in a large building as they look ineffective on paper. Four-part harmony is almost non-existent, and five-part sections for full choir are carefully spaced out at first, then gradually closed up as the work reaches its climax. The dynamic build-up is natural and logical throughout, a duo leading to a trio, which in turn expands into a five-part section. There are ample contrasts between few and many voices, and between high and low pitch, while the usefulness of the scheme lies in the lengthy rests for the voices not employed in the different trios and duos. No voice is made to sing for too long at a stretch, and the five voice-parts are split up into some fifteen separate combinations during the course of the work, thus exploiting to the full not only the range but the depth of vocal colour inherent in even a small choir. The counterpoint is non-imitative, in the best Franco-Flemish tradition, and gains its impetus by the incessant weaving of flexible and volatile melodic patterns. Melismatic passages occur from time to time throughout the entire work, but their extended use is restricted to the full sections, and of course the final *Amen*. The cantus firmus, *Justi in perpetuum vivent*, suggests a performance at Vespers on the Feast of Relics or of All Saints, both of which were classed as Greater Doubles in the Sarum Kalendar.

Byrd's antiphon is also designed to be

sung at Vespers, but the feast (as shown by the text) is that of Pentecost. There is no cantus firmus, and no reliance on plainsong. Each significant phrase, or even word, is given its own clearly recognizable theme, whilst the word *Alleluia* occurs continually in varying melodic garb, often forming counterpoint, invertible at the fifth or octave, with the other themes. At certain points *Alleluia* appears as a refrain, until new themes and a new fragment of the text take over and run their course. Imitation is, as a rule, quite strict and usually very close, but the themes are chosen and contrived in such a way as to impose no waywardness or lack of balance in the harmonic scheme, which is for the most part simple and unsophisticated. Rests are usually quite short, giving just sufficient time for the singers to snatch a breath; the result is that the five-voiced texture is practically continuous, although there is a certain sense of ebb and flow, of constant renewal of vocal and musical resources, which gives the work its drive and its noble sonority. Melismas occur, as indeed they should, on the closing *Alleluia,* and the spacing of the voices at the climax proves Byrd a consummate master of choral textures.

MUSIC FOR THE
ENGLISH RITE

IV

*F*ORTUNATELY
for the Elizabethans, religious music set to
English texts had almost as long a tradition
as Latin church music, although the main
difference between the two was in bulk.
Due mainly to the carol, English texts appeared alongside Latin ones in nearly all
the important manuscript sources, and if
the contention that the carol was proces-
sional music has the support of scholars,
it is not unreasonable to find in it the beginnings of vernacular polyphony. For
the average Plantagenet carol is no more
highly contrapuntal than the anthems and
services composed during the first two decades of the reign of Elizabeth: it was only

the intervening period spanned by Henry
VII and Henry VIII that saw the true
zenith of Tudor polyphony, majestic to the
point of extravagance, and sublimely indifferent to the audibility of the texts.

Even Tudor carols, with all their devotion to the then current melismata, began
to show strong traces of a new outlook in
the manner of setting words. Composers
took great care about the text being audible
at its first appearance. Once enunciated
(often with a syllable to a note), it is
allowed to merge into vocalization, and the
texture, from a lone utterance such as that
which opens Cornysch's *Woefully arrayed,*
becomes at once more dense and more mo-
tet-like. The earliest music for the English
rite was composed towards the very end of
Henry VIII's reign, and although it lacks
the striking solos and delectable duos of its
immediate precursors, it has a unique character through being neither wholly chordal
(like certain carols and para-liturgical
works) nor completely contrapuntal in the

way that some of Byrd's mature English anthems are.

The answer to those who maintain that late Henrician works are tentative and un-original is not that their composers were intimidated by Cranmerian principles, nor that they were the fruits of an imperfect technique. A composer of the standing of Tallis, who had filled the lofty vaults of Waltham Abbey with the massive sonority of a forty-part motet or a canonically in-tricate *Miserere* would hardly boggle at a straightforward piece of four-part harm-ony, note-against-note in the main. One would expect a dignified composition, out-wardly simple, yet full of cunning part-writing and careful spacing of voice-parts, breathing to a quiet rhythmic pulse by no means lacking in fine and subtle touches. This, indeed, is what often did result from these early experiments in harmonizing texts from Henry VIII's *Prymer* of 1545. But apart from a few published examples, they are insufficiently well known, often through the lack of a single part-book, whose absence has acted in some measure as a deterrent to inveterate transcribers.

It is frequently stated that the two halves of the sixteenth century were connected musically across the gulf which separated Elizabeth's broad Protestantism and Henry VIII's even broader Catholicism. This is only a half-truth, however, for the continuity that undoubtedly existed was a musico-technical one, and not musico-liturgical. The emphasis placed on this point is necessary in order to dispel the false but widespread idea that "the motet corresponded to the anthem, and the Mass to the Service." The motet, as has already been shown, was a term loosely applied to polyphonic music for the choir office and the Proper of the Mass. The Elizabethan anthem, designed to follow the Third Collect at Morning and Evening Prayer "in Quires and Places where they sing" was, as the Prayer Book tells us, by no means an essential part of the liturgy. It was a pleasant adornment to the ceremony, but one which could easily be dispensed with. The so-called "motet" could not be dispensed with unless plainsong took its place. Similarly, the Mass and the Service no more correspond with one another than do the anthem and the motet. Composers in England set four sections of the Ordinary of the Mass, and after the Reformation, when it became the custom to compose Services, a small but important number of these same composers found that their task included the setting to music of a wide variety of liturgical texts: Preces, Venite, Te Deum, Benedictus, Responses, Litany, Kyrie, Creed, Sanctus, Gloria, Magnificat, and Nunc Dimittis.

The Service, then, in its fullest form, was a compound of choral music for the Communion, and for Morning and Evening Prayer; it cannot be said to derive from the Mass in any way, apart from the superficial act of translation from Latin into English. The great majority of Elizabethan Services included only Kyrie and Creed as choral

music for the Communion: of these the
Kyrie was normally a choral version of the
responses to the Ten Commandments, and
not a tripartite structure as it had been in
the Sarum rite, or in the late Henrician
English Masses. This change in the nature
of the Kyrie took place at the same time as
the removal of the Gloria to the end of the
Communion, and was enforced by the
Prayer Book of 1552. The extreme Protestantism of Edward VI's reign may have
been partly responsible for the musical setting of only Kyrie and Creed, since the remaining sections (Sanctus and Benedictus,
Agnus Dei, and Gloria) occurred during
the latter and more solemn part of the
Communion service, when music was probably frowned upon. It is certainly noticeable that pre-Edwardian music for the
Communion service, like the later Elizabethan settings, tended to include the entire
number of texts whose choral performance
was approved by tradition. This is certainly true of the Communion services in

the Wanley part-books, which are usually dated 1546-47. Of ten complete services, only three omit the Kyrie, and even then the remainder of the texts are set, and even amplified by harmonized versions of the Offertory Sentences or the Postcommunion. More significant still is that one of these ten services, by Heath, was printed by Day in *Certaine Notes . . . . . to be sung at the Mornyng Communion* (1560), but without Benedictus and Agnus Dei. In similar fashion the greatest of the Elizabethan Communion settings, including those by Byrd (both the Short and Great Services) and by Richard Farrant and Thomas Morley, contain only Kyrie and Creed.

Notable exceptions to this procedure are the two best-known settings by Tallis. The so-called Dorian Service has a predominantly syllabic, though occasionally florid texture. Such florid passages as do occur are mostly confined to the inner parts at cadences. The part-writing, however, is of a highly competent order, and effective and sonorous within its limits. There is even a hint, in certain sections, of a head-motive—a mere four-note group—which may indicate that Tallis tried to retain some vestige of the cyclic form prevalent in his Latin music. It is to the credit of Tallis that he avoids monotony in spite of the epigrammatic, chant-like treatment of the individual items, and the chordal nature of the harmonization. At least two other services of his must at one time have existed in complete form: the bass part of one (preserved in the library of St. John's College, Oxford) proves that it was a full Service of very considerable proportions. The indication "of five parts, two in one" implies, moreover, that two of the parts were in canon for most if not all of the time. An English Te Deum, also of five parts, almost certainly comes from another Service which would have included music for the Communion.

Farrant's Service, as already mentioned, contains only two sections of the Communion: Kyrie and Creed. They echo certain of Tallis's stylistic features, and (like his music) could perfectly well be sung by men, since the uppermost part is fairly low in tessitura. Byrd's Short Service breaks new ground by breaking up the texture and contrasting various combinations of voice-parts. There are, it is true, paired entries from time to time in Farrant's Service, but the idea of contrast in texture is carried no further than this. With Byrd the procedure is fairly complex, and results in a welcome enlargement of expressive qualities and in effectual dynamic range. The Creed, as set by Byrd, even extends certain delicate hints (already apparent in Tallis and Farrant) of word-painting, especially at the phrases *And the third day He rose again . . . . and ascended into heaven.* Comparable treatment of this portion of the text may be seen in the Great Service, which makes the fullest use of antiphonal effects.

Antiphonal singing was not always appreciated during the early part of Elizabeth's reign, and the complex structure of the verse anthem which came into vogue well before the end of the sixteenth century can have done little to assuage the wrath of the Puritans, for whom it was a willful continuation of pre-Reformation practices. A London clergyman named John Field even went so far as to write *An Admonition to the Parliament* in 1572, criticizing the Anglican Service where "there is no edification, according to the Rule of the Apostle, but confusion; they tosse the Psalmes in most places like tennice-balls." Edward Hake, writing in Daman's *Psalmes of David* (1579) talks with equal feeling of the "over curious, yea, and as I may say over tragicall dismembring not onely of wordes but of letters and sillables in the holy Psalmes and Anthemes appointed to the praysing of God." If all this were true of psalm settings, it must have been equally true of music for the Communion services as sung in cathedrals and the Chapel

Royal, designated as "popyshe dennes" and "patternes . . . . of all superstition," in the tract written by Field. Fortunately for the Anglican Church, there were men of the calibre and integrity of John Case, who replied to these detractors by emphasizing the place which antiphonal singing held in the earliest days of the Christian Church, as well as in the Jewish ritual. There is, moreover, no clear evidence that those who criticized the Anglican way of singing had any sound alternative to offer. John Marbeck's *Booke of Common Praier Noted,* published in 1550, had failed to arouse any enthusiasm, although its quasi-mensural notation of unison chant should have satisfied the most ardent among reformers. It may well have been that its superficial resemblance to plainsong counted against its formal adoption by the adherents of four-part harmony and strict homophony. It is nevertheless interesting to compare the rhythmical schemes adopted by Marbeck in his setting of the Creed with exactly similar passages in Tallis's Dorian Service. There are enough coincidences to suggest that Tallis must have known Marbeck's music even before it came to be printed.

The canticles for Morning and Evening Service were less subject to change than the component parts of the Communion service, and a composer working on English texts from 1545 onwards would have had only changes of translation and phraseology to contend with, instead of the changing order of events in the Communion service, and the attendant confusion over what to include and what not to include. The grouping of Magnificat and Nunc Dimittis is found five times in the Wanley manuscripts, and besides these there is one separate and apparently unattached setting of Magnificat. Of the four groupings of morning canticles (Te Deum and Benedictus) two have a Venite also; and once again there is a separate Venite which, like the Magnificat, appears not to belong to any of the other groups. One of the sets of Evening canticles is probably the work of Tye (the Nunc Dimittis is attributed to him in another, and fortunately complete set of part-books) who with Tallis was among the first to attempt an intelligent solution of the problems posed by the Anglican liturgy. Another Evening service formerly attributed to Tye is now known to be the work of Osbert Parsley, sometime lay-clerk of Norwich Cathedral. Byrd, whose Short and Great Services have done so much to enhance his reputation, left two sets of Evening canticles which deserve to be better known. One is an early pioneer of the Verse Service, with passages for solo voice accompanied by the organ; the other, largely in triple time, contains subtle harmonic colours and an ingenious use of canon. Links between Magnificat and Nunc Dimittis were not frequent in Elizabethan settings, although there is a slight resemblance between the opening of the two canticles in Byrd's Short Service, and a definite duplication of material in

Farrant's Benedictus and Nunc Dimittis. If thematic connections between the music for Morning and Evening Prayer seem extraordinary, similar links between great Elizabethan composers in their different versions of Te Deum must be admitted to be an artistic commonplace. The most interesting example of this is to be found in the melodic material used for the words *Holy, Holy, Holy, Lord God of Sabaoth.* Byrd, Farrant, Tallis, and Bevin make use of exactly the same phrase for these words: a descending scale-segment of four notes, falling from the mediant to the leading-note of a minor scale.

Most composers naturally made the best use possible of the contrasts of tone which came from the division of the choir. Those singing on the side of the Dean's stall (Decani) were thus able to answer or join with an equivalent group on the north side (Cantoris) so called because of the Precentor's stall. It must be stressed that this English practice was in no way reliant upon the traditions of polychoralism, whose most important function apart from antiphony was the creation of a richer texture when the two choirs combined. Decani and Cantoris sides both consisted of S.A.T.B. groups which, when they coincided, usually sang exactly the same notes, resulting in an increase of volume rather than an increase in the density of the polyphonic texture. The introduction of verses for soloists, however, gave innumerable opportunities for complex and subtle interchanges of register, timbre, and volume; and it was due to the development of this technique by Byrd and Morley that the most prolific of Elizabethan composers of Services, Thomas Weelkes, came to contrive his magnificent Evening canticles for seven voices. Four altos are needed for the performance of this work, which has survived in a form enough complete for a reconstruction to be made. In richness and resource it is perhaps without parallel in the whole of the Elizabethan repertory, for Weelkes's ingenuity in marshalling his kaleidoscopic verse sections is only matched by the seven-part writing of the full sections for S.S.A.-A.T.B.B.

At least nine other Services by Weelkes are known to exist in fairly complete form, and they range from a normal four-part setting of "Short Service" stature to Verse Services of generous proportions and fine workmanship. Tomkins, whose work (like that of Gibbons) is really outside the scope of this survey, wrote at least seven Services, most of them being of the Verse type. Gibbons's Verse Service is generally thought to be less convincing musically than his Short Service, which is one of his best-known and most frequently sung compositions. Of Shepherd's three Services, only one—for tunately an excellent and vigorous speci-men—is complete. It proves that its author, like his contemporary Tallis, was in no way restricted by the insistence on simplicity in liturgical music: indeed, it seems rather to have acted as a spur in the creation of a fresh and clarified polyphonic outlook. This outlook was certainly shared by William Munday and Robert Parsons in their Services, while lesser names such as Nathaniel Patrick, John Amner, John Holmes, and Nathaniel Giles give ready proof of a widespread respect for this new and healthy musical texture, with its fine balance between counterpoint and homophony.

It is often difficult to realize that alongside this intensive pursuit of church music for its own sake (for there were no outlets worth speaking of in the world of printing and publishing) the choirs were often badly looked after, meagrely rewarded for their services, and much reduced in numbers. The economic position in England had steadily deteriorated throughout the reign of Henry VIII, and its effect on musical establishments is only too readily apparent in contemporary allusions to choirs. In Roger Ascham's *Toxophilus* (1545) one of the characters, or rather interlocutors, bewails the unhappy state of musical education, wishing "that the laudable custom of England to teach children their pricksong, were not so decayed throughout all the realm as it is." Twenty years later the position was still as bad, if we are to believe the retrospective musings of an anonymous seventeenth-century writer on church music. It is his contention that "the first occasion of the decay of Musick in Cathedrall Churches and other places, where musick and singing was used and had yearly allowance began about the ninth yeare of Queene Elizabeth."

The fact was that retrenchments of one kind or another—not only in the "yearly allowance"—had been taking place steadily through the troubled reigns of Edward and Mary, and the damage done to the structure of cathedral music was serious enough to create a continuing weakness in what should have been a strong national tradition. One method of making ends meet involved the reduction of num-

bers in the choir, so that the fixed amount
of money could be divided among fewer
people. Another method was to import
men from the city to the cathedral at a low
salary, as at Canterbury in 1560, where the
statutory number of twelve minor canons
could not otherwise be maintained. The
organist or master of the children was often
hard hit by economic difficulties, for more
often than not he had to provide for the
children's board and lodging as well as
teach them daily. In 1583, William Hun-
nis, then Master of the Children of the
Chapel Royal, petitioned for an increase
in allowances, which was not apparently
granted. Complaining of the difference between "the prices of things present to the
time past" he says: "the burden hereof
hath from time to time so hindered the
masters of the children viz. Master Bower,
Master Edwardes, myself and Master Farrant: that notwithstanding some good
helps otherwise some of them died in so
poor case, and so deeply indebted that

they have not left scarcely wherewith to bury them." Yet there was good spirit among the community of musicians as a whole. They struggled gallantly to maintain what was, to them, a worthwhile tradition of composition and performance; and their music, having little or no commercial value—unlike its continental counterpart—was a means to a spiritual end. "The better the voice is," said William Byrd, "the meeter it is to honour and serve God therewith: and the voice of man is chiefly to be employed to that end."

The new liturgical reforms, however, were concerned not only with the voice of man but the voice of many: the sharing in certain parts of the service; notably the psalms, which any musical congregation might be expected to approve. Music was slow, at first, to appear in the many published psalters, and the harmonizations were understandably functional rather than artistic — an attribute which remained throughout the succeeding centuries, and which caused the eminent Bohemian composer, Dvorak, to ask why the choir of St. Paul's Cathedral persisted in repeating a bad tune so often. Oddly enough, some of the best Tudor psalm-tunes, those written by Thomas Tallis for Archbishop Parker's Psalter, were never circulated in their own time, since the Psalter was printed but never placed on sale. The composers of the tunes in Sternhold and Hopkins's Psalter of 1562 are unknown; but the thirty additional tunes given in the Day Psalter, published in the following year, were the work of men such as Thomas Caustun and William Parsons. Psalmody during the last two decades of the century received further stimulus from varied publications by Allison, Byrd, Cosyn, Daman, Denham, and East. East's *Whole Booke of Psalmes* (1592) contains settings by ten or more composers; Allison's *Psalmes of David in Metre,* however, consists entirely of his own work. A few composers, notably Tallis, Byrd, Morley, and Gibbons, set parts of psalms for special festivals in a manner which was akin to chanting, yet more florid and interesting than straightforward chants. These versions were given the name of *Psalmi Festivales,* a term which was wide enough to include even a rudimentary "Verse Anthem" type such as Byrd's *Teach me O Lord,* set out for full choir alternating with solo voice and organ.

Psalm texts were, of course, greatly in demand for anthems of all types. Byrd included ten five-part Psalms in his publication *Psalms, Sonets and Songs* (1588), and may himself have been responsible for the English adaptation of *Attollite portas,* from *Cantiones Sacrae* of 1575, which became widely known as *Lift up your heads*. It is not always possible to attribute arrangements and adaptations to the original composer, even if it is assumed that his approval would have extended so far. Yet many anthems current in Elizabethan times were direct arrangements of motets. Some even inspired two separate texts: Taver-

ner's *In nomine* (not really a motet, but
part of his Mass *Gloria tibi Trinitas*) provided the musical structure for an anthem,
published in Day's *Certaine notes . . . .*
(1560). The text of this version was *In
trouble and adversitie,* whereas a contemporary manuscript using the same music
has an English setting which begins *O give
thanks unto the Lord.* Two well-known anthems by Tallis, *O sacred and holy banket*
and *I call and cry* are both adapted from *O
sacrum convivium,* and the same composer's *Absterge Domine* gave rise to two anthems (*Wipe away my sins* and *Discumfit
them O Lord*) the latter of which has often,
wrongly, been associated with the defeat
of the Spanish Armada. In both cases it
will be noticed that one of the texts bears
some relation to the Latin original: the
other is separate and unrelated. Later
editors and collectors, including Aldrich,
Boyce, and Oliphant, made numerous
adaptations of motets; but having grafted
on an English text they often disposed of

the Latin one so completely that an accurate reference is a matter of some difficulty. The close connection between psalm and motet may be seen in the versions of Tallis's *O Lord in thee is all my trust* and *Remember not O Lord God,* as they appear in Day's *Certaine notes . . .* and *The Whole Psalmes* which followed three years later. In both cases the latter version is much abridged.

Day was the first English publisher of anthems, and although his books must have served the public well, there was no comparison between the cost of copying an anthem by hand, and the cost of publication. Consequently there were few successors to Day's venture in the field of liturgical music until long after the close of Elizabeth's reign. Byrd's collections of vocal and instrumental pieces contained secular items in addition to psalms and works with sacred texts, while the *Teares or Lamentacions of a Sorrowfull Soule,* published in 1614 by Sir William Leighton, had exclusively religious texts but a pointedly secular style of instrumentation. The majority of late Tudor anthems are therefore preserved at first hand in manuscript sources only, and did not reach the printing press until John Barnard's *First Book of Selected Church Musick* (1641).

The earliest type of full anthem was never so called: the term "full" was introduced at a later date in contrast to "verse." Nor indeed was the full anthem invariably written throughout for full choir. The normal division on *decani* and *cantoris* sides of the choir resulted in antiphonal singing in anthems as well as in Services, so that for the greater part of the time the full strength of the choir was not being used. A few modern editions still fail to take this antiphonal practice into account, even when it is most explicit in the music itself. Tye's four-part *I will exalt Thee* is a case in point. Both Tye and Shepherd left a small but distinguished collection of anthems, of which fourteen from each composer have come down to us. Of Tallis's work, seventeen anthems are now recoverable. Some of these, for example *If ye love me,* are to be sung antiphonally; others like *Purge me O Lord* are straightforward "full" settings, varying from quasi-syllabic works to contrapuntal structures of considerable elaboration.

There are numerous liturgical anthems by Okeland, Caustun, Johnson, Shepherd, and Whitbroke in the Wanley manuscripts and in sources contemporary with them, and it is much to be regretted that these unique early sources are often incomplete. Concordances increase in later Tudor times, with the result that a fair number of anthems by Parsons, Byrd, Farrant, White, and their fellow-composers is recoverable, thereby illuminating the high degree of technical equipment possessed by the best men of the Elizabethan school of church musicians. The later group, including not only Weelkes, Gibbons, and Tomkins but also Byrd (who lived on until

1623) were all enthusiastic supporters of the Verse Anthem, although it is often hinted that their compositions in this vein cannot bear comparison with their other works. The "verses," so named perhaps after the verses of psalms which had originally been used for texts, gave soloists an opportunity to shine, and the number of solo voices needed would vary from one to six, occasionally even more. Verses were usually accompanied on the organ, and parts for this instrument were often sketched out for the use of the player. If no organ were to hand, viols could be (and often were) used to good effect, especially in anthems suitable for performance in a private room or chapel.

There is no doubt that the musical vigour of the anthem, as an art-form, had few rivals in Elizabethan times. It retained that vigour, in changing forms, until the death of Purcell, but its highest peaks were topped well before the end of the sixteenth century.

THE ROLE PLAYED
BY INSTRUMENTS

V

*I*T WOULD BE
wrong indeed to think of Tudor church
music as an exclusively vocal culture, even
though the form in which it is usually made
available—either as printed text or as actual sound—pays scant regard to instrumental participation. There is no doubt
that, at certain times during the Tudor
epoch, instruments played an important
role in music performed in cathedrals, college chapels, and of course the Chapel
Royal. At other times, notably those years
when reforming zeal was at its height, there
was a grave danger that even the most
hallowed of all ecclesiastical wind instruments, the organ, would be forever ban-

ished and silenced. Fortunately the danger was averted, and both organs and organists suffered less than they did in the time of the Commonwealth. But the official outlook, as expressed in the second *Tome of Homelyes,* published in 1563 and appointed "to be read in eurey paryshe Churche agreablye," referred to the piping, singing, chanting and playing upon the organs as "things which displeased God so sore, and filthily defiled his holy house and place of prayer." Extreme views of this kind did not go unchallenged, however, thanks to the existence of a small but influential group of reasonable persons in the universities and cathedral cities. One such person, John Case of Oxford, published an elaborate and plausible defence of church music in *The Praise of Music* (1586) where he is careful to emphasize Biblical traditions.

"But the holy Ghost, the author of the Psalms, appointed and commanded them by the prophet *David,* to be song, and to be song most cunningly, and to be song with diverse artificiall instruments of Musick, and to bee song with sundry severall, and most excellent notes and tunes." Case concludes that the English church is completely justified in thus performing the psalms. Commenting a few pages later on the attitude towards organ playing he voices his disapproval of the men who "at the reading of the chapters should walke in the bodie of the church, and when the Organ play, give attentive heed thereunto: as if the whole and better part of the service did consist in Musick." That Case was able to make such a reservation proves that musical awareness had progressed considerably in a fairly short time, for only a decade before his book was published an exactly opposite attitude was rife: "few or none of the people would vouchsafe to come into the Quyres during the singinge service but would stand without, dauncinge and sportinge themselves until the sermons and lectures did begin, scorning and derydinge both the service and those which were imployed therein . . . ."

Before considering in detail the place of the organ in pre- and post-Reformation liturgies, it is significant to note the frequent incursions of other instruments, from the time of the cantus firmus Mass and motet to the beginnings of the verse anthem. There are unfortunately no early English pictorial proofs of the familiar scene of singers and players gathered around a large choir-book, supported on a lectern, although there are many continental examples. Usually these woodcuts or engravings show such instruments as the cornett and the slide trumpet, these two instruments between them having the three-octave compass required by full-scale motets and Masses. The lack of illustrations in England is to some extent remedied by royal and capitular accounts which frequently mention players of the cornett or the sackbut. Many of these players were full members of the musical establishment, and were held to be so important that on one occasion the income from a certain benefice was even diverted so that the cathedral could continue to enjoy its wind instrumentalists. When ingenious devices like this were either impossible or inadvisable, musicians were hired for special occasions from the town waits—skilled groups of players whose primary function as guardians and watchmen of the municipality was slowly being replaced by a new role bound up with official entertainments.

The tone of the cornett, when well played, was said to resemble very nearly the timbre of the human voice: thus it was an ideal instrument for the accompaniment or doubling of choral forces. Similarly, the slide trumpet (or sackbut, as it was called) gave excellent results in the hands of a skilled performer, and its considerable agility combined with possibilities of fine intonation and expert blend made it an admirable partner for the cornett. In addition, it was a tower of strength in the

117

sustaining of long tenor cantus firmi, for although these were often conventionally underlaid with words, their long notes and even longer phrases marked them out as material rather for playing than for singing, although both voices and instruments could (and at times did) join forces. Tenors of this type, in the early part of the fifteenth century, were often split up between two similar instruments, in order to give the players time to take in a fresh breath: *tenor* and *contratenor* would thus be complementary. A *solus tenor* was usually written down as a safeguard, and this would consist of a combination of the other two parts, with no breathing spaces at all, unless of course the isorhythmic pattern made allowance for them. A conflate of *tenor* and *contratenor,* called *solus tenor,* indicates the use of the organ, and we may therefore assume that two methods existed for performance of Mass sections and motets: one with organ alone, and the other with a consort of instruments. By the last two decades of the fifteenth century, the organ, as an accompanying instrument, may have been ousted by the cornett-sackbut team, since the long, unbroken type of tenor had become extremely rare. The steady development of organ technique was soon to equip it for a new and more important role in the liturgy. But the other instruments remained, much to the annoyance of the purists, and it is no surprise to hear of Erasmus complaining about "horns, trumpets and pipes constantly accompanying and alternating with the voices." This is just the kind of performance commented upon by the Italian visitor mentioned in an earlier chapter, and it was probably very fashionable up to 1525 or 1530, when the Tudor organists began to exploit their newly-coined techniques of elaborating plainsong.

During Elizabeth's reign, the pendulum swung back once more in favour of wind instruments, which we find accompanying the Queen on her royal visits to Worcester and Oxford. The Oxford visit took place in 1566, and a commendably careful observer tells us that the Queen "entered into the church, and there abode, while the quyer sang and play'd with cornetts *Te Deum*." The next year, at Ely, we find an early reference to the teaching of the viol, which suggests that choristers were then beginning to learn an instrument which was something of a novelty to them: yet this same instrument was destined to be accepted as the finest type of accompaniment for the verse anthem, so that the long supremacy of wind instruments was at last threatened, though never completely shaken.

The supremacy of the organ, and indeed of organ music, dates from the middle of Henry VIII's reign and extends to 1547, the year in which John Redford died. From there onwards it is connected by various subterranean streams to the vast output of Thomas Tomkins, who probably began his compilation of organ books—most of which are now lost—towards the very end of Elizabeth's reign. There is no evidence that organ music was published in England at any time during the period under review: everything composed was written down and passed on in manuscript form, much of which must have been lost or destroyed. In the history of organ music under the Tudors, there is a certain feeling of continuity rather akin to that which was apparent in the choral music. The link, in this instance, is the Offertory; the one point in the Mass or Communion Service where the organist could indulge his flights of fancy or improvisation. One of the earliest among many Offertory settings still in existence is the *Felix namque* in a fifteenth century manuscript in the Bodleian library. This short, two-part composition, based on a variant of the familiar *Felix namque* plainsong, shows the inventive and decorative faculties at work in a simple yet effective way. When, at the other extreme of the Tudor dynasty, we find references to

Dr. Bull "at the organ playing the Offertory" during an Easter Communion Service at court, it is tempting to think that the same plainsong was being used for the same purpose well over a hundred years later than the Bodleian fragment.

The organ Offertory shows, perhaps more clearly than any other musicoliturgical form, the precise impact of the Reformation on Tudor composers. The earliest custom demanded that the priest or celebrant should intone the opening of the Offertory, just as in a monophonic choral interpretation. But at the point where the chorus would normally enter, the organ began to play, and still keeping to the plainsong (or a variant at one remove, such as a faburden) embellished it with a constantly changing pattern of counterpoint and imitation. Settings by Redford (*Precatus est Moyses, Justus ut palma, Felix namque*), John Thorne of York (*Exsultabunt sancti*), Thomas Preston of St. George's, Windsor (*Reges Thar-*

sis, Diffusa est gratia, Felix namque, Confessio) all show these same features. Yet both Preston and Philip ap Rhys (who, like Redford, was an organist at St. Paul's Cathedral) wrote irregular settings of Offertories, in which the priest's intonation is also set for the organ. This treatment recalls the post-Reformation settings by Tallis of *Felix namque,* where the intonation is not only set but is even repeated.

The mention of the term *faburden,* derived from fauxbourdon, calls for an explanation not only because of its wide use among the Tudor organists, but also because the technique of composition to which it refers is often misunderstood. The method of producing a faburden to a given plainsong was fundamentally quite simple and straightforward: a part, moving note against note with the plainsong, was written below it at the distance of a sixth or an octave. For obvious reasons sixths predominated, but octave intervals were generally used at the opening and close, and occasionally during the course of the piece; this constituted, in effect, the skeleton of a regular fauxbourdon, as it would have been composed for vocal performance. But at this point there is a divergence in method. Where the composer of a choral faux-bourdon would add an extra part moving a perfect fourth below the plainsong, thus creating chains of 6-3 chords, the organist would do away entirely with the original plainsong, retaining only the faburden. This he would use as both bass and basis of his contrapuntal superstructure. The reason for doing this rather than using the original melody may be seen in the slightly more angular, functional-bass patterns of the faburden. Its harmonic implications were stronger than those of the plainsong, and it was thus peculiarly fitted to be used as a cantus firmus in the bass. Later generations of organists occasionally moved it into the treble register—Blitheman does so in his *Te Deum*—but this is a comparatively rare procedure. The title "upon the faburden" is sometimes present as an appendage to the title of the plainsong itself, but its omission does not indicate that the music has not been based on a faburden.

It will be recalled that Erasmus, in his complaint about instrumental music in church, mentioned the alternation of instruments with voices. This age-old principle of antiphony lies at the root of nearly all the surviving organ music from Henry VIII's reign. In very few cases is the music complete on its own: it must always be arranged so that intervening verses can be sung in unison by a choir, either of men's voices alone, or of boys and men singing in octaves. Only then does the pattern of hymn, Magnificat, Mass, and Te Deum become clear to the modern listener.

Hymn verses were among the most frequently written items in the liturgical organist's repertoire. They outnumber by far even the great number of settings of the antiphon *Miserere mihi Domine*. The largest collection of hymn verses is to be found in a manuscript dating from Redford's time: indeed there are many of his compositions in it, although it is no longer thought that some of the music is in his own handwriting. A hymn like *Salvator mundi Domine,* which usually has five verses, is given three organ verses in this manuscript, and the inference is that the organist played verses 1, 3, and 5, and the choir sang verses 2 and 4. *Christe qui lux,* which has seven verses in all, has an organ version with four verses, presumably 1, 3, 5, and 7. The melody would always be present in the organ setting, although it was not always audible as such. Faburden might cover up its familiar contour, or (retaining its original shape) it might be absorbed into the texture by subtle and remarkable decoration. Then again, it might disappear from the aural perspective by clinging to one of the inner parts, as in the last three verses of Redford's *Christe qui lux.* Only very exceptionally

126

did the melody rise to the treble voice-part, although it does so proudly in the middle verse of an anonymous *Iste confessor,* and the last verse of Blitheman's *Eterne rerum conditor.* At the beginning of an important, though anonymous collection of hymns ranged in the order of the Christian year, Thomas Tomkins (a former owner of this same manuscript) has written "all these are uppon the faburden of these playnsongs." There are twenty complete hymns, beginning at *Conditor alme siderum* (for Advent) until *Audi benigne conditor,* a Lenten hymn, as is the unfinished twenty-first hymn *Ecce tempus idoneum.* All these show a mature and meticulous outlook on problems of setting plainsong, and in many the results are so fine that, to quote Morley, "one not very well skilled in music should scant discern any plainsong whatsoever."

Antiphons were less frequently taken by the organists, although there are two noble settings of *Lucem tuam* (the antiphon to

Nunc Dimittis at Compline in the feast of the Holy Trinity), one by Redford, and the other by Richard Winslade, who was organist of Winchester Cathedral in the early part of the sixteenth century. The two versions of *Glorificamus te Dei genitrix* are both anonymous, but they may well be the work of John Redford, whose fine four-part elaboration of this antiphon (found in the Mulliner Book) shows his particular regard for its florid yet solemn character. The great number of *Miserere* settings is explained by the fact that this antiphon was so often used at Compline. A Sarum rubric enjoins the singing of the antiphon upon the Compline psalms "throughout Advent, and from the morrow of the Octave of the Epiphany to Quadragesima, and from Sunday in the Passion of the Lord up to the Supper of the Lord, and from the morrow of the Feast of Trinity to Advent, except in Feasts, and in the Octave of the Blessed Mary, and in the Feast of the Relics, and of All Saints." Quite obviously, many and varied settings were desirable.

Te Deum, the hymn of St. Ambrose and St. Augustine, is always set out in alternating fashion, just as the shorter and more metrical hymns are. When Henry VII visited York at the very beginning of the sixteenth century, the hymn was sung in the Minster in this way, and the organ may well have taken part, as it certainly did in the Chapel Royal when celebrations were ordered (in November 1554) for the reconciliation of England and the Church of Rome. One of the earliest settings is by Avery Burton, a member of the Chapel Royal in the early years of Henry VIII's reign, and it is worthy of note that he makes considerable use of ligatures in his organ verses. These notes bound together "in ligature" are more often found in vocal than in instrumental music, though there is a distinct possibility that their continued use was due, in some measure, to a desire on the part of the organists to bring out finer points of phrasing. John Redford and

William Blitheman also set *Te Deum,* and displayed considerable agility in their handling of brilliant decoration and ornament. A constant striving after variety of mood and texture is shown by the frequent employment of passages in "proportion," or what would now be called 6/8 or 9/8 time. In addition to this, the position of the cantus firmus was subject to change just as much as the number of parts, so that in performance the organ verses appear to possess an almost kaleidoscopic range of colour and expression.

Only one example of a Magnificat for organ and plainsong has come down to us, though this canticle must often have been set by organists. No composer's name is given, though stylistic links (including a predilection for *alla zoppa* rhythms) suggest Avery Burton, whose *Te Deum* it immediately follows in the manuscript source. The piece is simply called "The viij tune in C fa ut," and is accordingly based on the faburden of the eighth tone, transposed to C. The next work in the same manuscript is just as unique though far more important. It is the only surviving complete example of an English organ Mass, a form which appears to have originated either in Italy or Germany, and was subsequently much developed in France. The composer is Philip ap Rhys, a Welsh organist who came to London and held posts at various city churches before his appointment to St. Paul's Cathedral. Rhys has set the whole of the Ordinary of the Mass, with the exception of the Credo (although there are indications that he intended to compose music for this, too) and he has also included an Offertory which tells us that the work was composed for the feast of the Holy Trinity. The Mass begins with a troped Kyrie *Deus creator omnium,* in which the organist supplies music for the first, third, fifth, seventh, and ninth invocations. *Gloria in excelsis* is likewise set in alternation, though the scheme on which the alternation is based is quite different

from any other continental organ Mass of
the time. The Offertory is an extensive yet
carefully-wrought setting of *Benedictus sit
Deus Pater,* which is proper to the feast.
Sanctus, Benedictus and Agnus Dei show
numerous Tudor characteristics in the matter of style and technique: there is a distinct liking for clear but ascetic counterpoint in two or three parts, coupled with
a fondness for melodic sequences and lin-
gering cadences which so frequently find
their vocal counterpart in the Henrician
and Elizabethan motet.

The only other comparable setting of a
large-scale liturgical canvas is by Thomas
Preston, who has given us an equally
unique example of the Proper of the Mass,
for Easter Sunday. Introit (*Resurrexi*),
Gradual (*Haec dies*), Alleluia with its
verses *Pascha nostrum* and *Epulemur,*
and Sequence (*Fulgens praeclara*) are all
based on the plainsongs or on the faburden. Preston, like Blitheman, was a brilliant player, and there is ample evidence

of his resourceful technique in this group of liturgical pieces for Easter. He was a prolific composer of Offertories, and has left eight different yet full-scale versions of *Felix namque*, besides one each of *Reges Tharsis* and *Diffusa est gratia*.

From the middle of the century onwards, organ music became less and less closely bound up with the liturgy. *Felix namque*, a long yet popular plainsong beloved of the organists, was slowly ousted by the rival claims of the "In nomine" which was sweeping through every musical field of activity, from grave consort music to gay and humorous settings of London street cries. The "In nomine" (usually referred to by its correct liturgical title of *Gloria tibi Trinitas*) soon invaded the organ loft, and we find no less than six versions, contained in one and the same manuscript, by William Blitheman. Although, strictly speaking, they do not come under the heading of liturgical organ music, they might well have been used in churches as opening or closing voluntaries. The term "Voluntary" came into use for the first time at roughly the same date as the vogue of the "In nomine." There are two voluntaries, widely different in both size and character, in the Mulliner Book, and the three examples by Byrd show that he, too, followed in the footsteps of Allwood and the elder Farrant. The idea of the voluntary as a free composition without any plainsong basis was fundamentally important, as it heralded the rapid development of fantasia technique which played so great a part in the instrumental music of the seventeenth century. But the organ fantasy remained relatively unimportant in England: for all its freedom from melodic ties, the voluntary, like the fantasy, remained unattractive to keyboard players. Even when they were so far removed from the Sarum rite that they could not even remember the name of the plainsong being used, they continued to use it because it gave them the structural basis which they found indispensable.

In view of the fluent and idiomatic keyboard style so typical of Byrd at his best, it is perhaps surprising to find that he ventured so rarely into the realms of liturgical organ music. His motets, Gradualia and Masses show him to be the kind of stalwart Catholic entirely content to compose music for a liturgy no longer current in his own country, and if he could cheerfully do this, it follows that he might well have written—if only for future use—a corpus of liturgical organ music comparable with that of the early Tudor composers. But what is most significant is that his teacher, Thomas Tallis, and his pupil, Thomas Tomkins, have both left a sizable collection of organ music: Byrd, in between the two, seems not to have thought along the same lines, unless (as has already been hinted) the Commonwealth period saw an end to as many organ books as organs.

Tallis's organ music proves that—apart from the two gigantic settings of *Felix namque*—vocal polyphony was uppermost in his mind, even when he was actually playing the organ, as undoubtedly he did at Waltham Abbey, Canterbury Cathedral, and the Chapel Royal. Apart from small cadential flourishes and incidental decoration of a discreet nature, there is very little evidence of an organ style even half as idiomatic as that of Redford, Preston, and Blitheman. There is, nevertheless, a gracious and contemplative atmosphere about the antiphons and hymn verses which make the listener curious to know more of the composer's keyboard music, and more especially organ music.

John Bull, who was a pupil of Blitheman, must have written many of his *Gloria tibi Trinitas* settings whilst in England. His other work, which dates from the period of his Antwerp post, falls outside the scope of this book, although it is more truly liturgical than the vigorous and remarkable pieces which appear in the Fitzwilliam Virginal Book, the Tomkins manuscript in the Paris Conservatoire, and other contemporary sources. One piece by Bull called both "In nomine" and "Kyrie eleison" in the Paris manuscript, is in fact neither: it is a setting of a hymn-tune, and thus has no connection with an organ Mass.

The still unchanged double-stave appearance of music right up to the time of Bull and Tomkins does not preclude the existence of a pedal organ any more than it implies inordinate stretching power in the hands of the organists. There is no doubt that a pedal register of 8 and 4 foot ranks would have been ideal for the performance of cantus firmi. Assuming a staid and dignified attitude to the technique of pedalling, the normal progression of a plainsong melody in semibreves or breves would have fitted such an attitude to perfection. Hands would be free to deal with passage-work which was often difficult enough on its own, without the bother of having to hold down a long note throughout a whole bar. But it is often noticeable that composers tended towards notational pessimism, and the thought that their works may have to be played on manuals alone explains why they often take such care to keep the cantus firmus, whenever possible, within the reasonable ambit of one pair of hands.

Much of the organ music of Thomas Tomkins, like that of Bull, belongs to the post-Elizabethan age; but it has its roots in the early school in more than one sense. Tomkins was a conservative in that he continued to use and exploit the forms known to the Henrician organists, and also to use—almost in copy-book fashion—the priceless manuscripts which had somehow been preserved from the orgy of reform and destruction. His comments, mostly marginal but none the less perspicacious, show him to be a true connoisseur and a fine musician. He knows how to sort out the good from the indifferent, and he corrects orthographical faults with the skill of a thoroughly experienced editor. His works are the final flowering of a great tradition.

EPILOGUE

VI

*I*N THE *RE-solves,* published in 1628, of Owen Feltham, there is a chapter about the nature and effects of music—a conventional chapter, for the most part, with all the accustomed allusions to musical practitioners both classical and mythological. One passage, however, shows that Feltham, in company with other literary men of his time, was not unwilling to make brief reference to his own experience of music: ". . . . I think hee hath not a *minde* well tempered, whose zeal is not inflamed by a *heavenly Anthem.* So that indeed *Musicke* is *good,* or *bad,* as the end to which it tendeth."

The history of Tudor church music shows us that its chief protagonists adopted an attitude which was largely consistent in its idealism and its principal aims. Music, for them, was no proselytizing vehicle, no inflamer of zeal for or against reform. It was an art whose function was to adorn and beautify the ceremonial of the church. Its character, as distinct from its style (which as we have seen, varied considerably within certain limits) embodied to the highest degree those features of repose and reverence without which no liturgical composition is truly complete. Above all, it must be remembered that music of this kind refuses to give up its secrets to those who are content merely to regard its physical aspect, whether in choirbooks, partbooks, or modern scores. It must be heard in conditions which are not only as nearly ideal as possible, but which reproduce exactly the liturgical framework—the *raison d'être* of the original composition.

Feltham's "heavenly Anthem" reached his ears through no ancillary medium of disc or radio, nor was it read in the silence of his study or reduced to comfortable dimensions by the sound of his clavichord. It was heard in some spacious cathedral or abbey, where sympathetic resonance minimized the faults and exaggerated the virtues of the performance as well as of the composition itself. In other words, the anthem became heavenly through its *milieu* rather than through any intrinsic power of its own, although a composer was naturally bound to present his ideas in such a way that the uplifting, as it were, of his musical offering caused no grave difficulties in execution and involved no unseemly display of vain or earth-bound talents.

As soon as extraneous elements appeared, whether personal or theatrical, attention was drawn from the service of the church to the surface of the music—to all those immediately apparent tricks of harmony, melody, and ornament which flatter and titillate the average ear. Such tricks were commonplaces of church music in England during the eighteenth and nineteenth centuries, and their pernicious influence can still be heard in churches and cathedrals today. Music written for the glorification of choir and organist cannot be other than "bad, as the end to which it tendeth." Neglect in avoiding the obvious has often led to the downright banal, so that a canticle intended for choir use, has (through its over-use and its inherent weakness) become ripe for congregational performance. Fortunately participation of this kind is out of the question as far as the Tudor repertory is concerned, except of course in psalm and hymn melodies intended for congregational use.

There is urgent need not only for a complete and integrated study of the entire corpus of Tudor church music, but for an increased knowledge of its treasures in those places where it would undoubtedly achieve the greatest good. There is no lack of variety in its wide span and its catholic embrace of forms and styles; in range alone it links the traditions of the Middle

Ages with the new outlook of the Baroque era. Without it the history, as well as the musical history, of England would be incalculably the poorer.